ERRATA

Page 94, caption: for *north*, read *south*

Page 134, caption: for *east*, read *southeast*

Page 155, caption: for *Adjoining of*, read *of Adjoining*

Page 162: picture is reversed

Page 377, caption: for *south*, read *north*

Page 466, item 478: for 1817, read 1878

Page 478, caption: for 1817, read 1878

Page 533, entry for Michelangelo Buonarroti: for 1474, read 1475

PRINTED IN HOLLAND

KEY

OF THE

OF

MONUMENTS

HISTORY

ARCHITECTURE

Edited by HENRY A. MILLON

ASSISTANT PROFESSOR, SCHOOL OF ARCHITECTURE AND PLANNING,

MASSACHUSETTS INSTITUTE OF TECHNOLOGY

TEXT EDITION

PRENTICE-HALL, INC., Englewood Cliffs, N.J.

AND

HARRY N. ABRAMS, INC., New York

Library of Congress Catalog Card Number: 64-10764
All rights reserved. No part of the contents of this book
may be reproduced without the written permission of the
publishers, Harry N. Abrams, Incorporated, New York

PRINTED AND BOUND IN HOLLAND

CONTENTS

PREFACE   7

I. THE ANCIENT WORLD

LIST OF ILLUSTRATIONS   11

1. Prehistoric and Primitive Architecture   17

2. Egyptian Architecture   23

3. Architecture of the Ancient Near East   40

4. Minoan and Mycenaean Architecture   51

5. Greek Architecture   57

6. Etruscan Architecture   86

7. Roman Architecture   89

8. Early Christian Architecture   121

9. Byzantine Architecture   134

II. ASIA AND AMERICA

LIST OF ILLUSTRATIONS   147

10. Islamic Architecture   149

11. Architecture of Indian Asia   162

12. Chinese and Japanese Architecture   167

13. American Architecture before Columbus   179

III. THE MIDDLE AGES

LIST OF ILLUSTRATIONS   191

14. Early Medieval Architecture   195

15. Romanesque Architecture   206

16. Gothic Architecture   232

17. Late Gothic Architecture   258

IV. THE RENAISSANCE

LIST OF ILLUSTRATIONS   293

18. Early Renaissance Architecture   301

19. High Renaissance Architecture   323

20. Sixteenth-Century Architecture in Italy   333

21. Sixteenth-Century Architecture outside Italy   355

22. Architecture of the Seventeenth-Century in Italy   373

23. Seventeenth-Century Architecture in France and England   393

24. Seventeenth-Century Architecture in Flanders, Holland, Spain, Germany, Austria, and the New World   412

25. Eighteenth-Century Architecture in Europe and the New World   422

V. THE MODERN WORLD

LIST OF ILLUSTRATIONS   466

26. Nineteenth-Century Architecture in England, France, and the United States of America   469

27. Nineteenth-Century Architecture in Austria, Belgium, Germany, Italy, and Holland   487

28. Twentieth-Century Architecture   494

INDEX OF PERSONS AND PLACES   531

LIST OF ABBREVIATED SOURCES   536

NOTE ON THE PICTURE CAPTIONS

Photographic sources accompany the captions in the List of Illustrations *that precedes each of the five parts of the book. Sources have been abbreviated in many cases, and the full citation will be found in the* List of Abbreviated Sources *on p. 536. Dates in the captions refer to buildings; biographical dates accompany architects' names in the* Index.

PREFACE

THIS VOLUME was conceived by the publishers as a companion to H. W. Janson's *Key Monuments of the History of Art*. As the architectural monuments selected by Professor Janson constitute most of the major achievements, virtually all those in his volume are included here. About this nucleus were grouped new selections, further plans, sections, and details. Additions were also made to provide a variety of protagonists or to outline the development of a structural system or a spatial ideal. There are further additions designed to produce the setting in which the major architectural achievements play their roles; bridges, sewers, defensive walls, roads, and other engineering works serve as flats and props. Furthermore, it is usually within a city or at least within a complex of buildings that a key monument is constructed. For this reason I have included a number of city plans (when possible and pertinent they chronicle the stages of development of the city) not so much for their intrinsic merit as to define the theater as a whole. A number of the inclusions may be thought by some to be peripheral, but the significance of a work of architecture, however exhilarating it may be as an isolated object, rests in its setting within a well-defined social and visual environment.

The history of architecture is concerned with buildings—large and small—singly or in groups, in natural or man-made surroundings; with the construction and function of the building; with the esthetic, social, and philosophical bases upon which a building may be founded; and with the structural and decorative systems employed to achieve desired spatial and esthetic goals. A collection of visual material for the study of the history of architecture must therefore provide information about spatial sequences, light sources and quality, exterior and interior mass form, structure, and surface articulation. A plan and section with interior and exterior photographs supply only the bare skeleton. A full description necessitates additional sections, plans at various levels, and photographs of the exterior and interior taken from numerous points of view and at different times of day to indicate varying light quality. These multiple requirements make the collection of visual material for the history of architecture an exacting task.

If each work were to be covered adequately, the 700–800 illustrations at my disposal would allow no more than 100–150 buildings. I have sought instead to select for reasonable coverage at least one outstanding example from each period. With these examples other monuments may be compared and contrasted. In this way I was able to include some 425 works.

Manuscripts, mosaics, engravings, or drawings are the only remaining record of some architectural monuments. Other buildings are known only through archaeological techniques that have uncovered foundation plans, located remains revealing ruined structures, and identified fragments incorporated into later buildings. All non-extant buildings require

reconstructions. These reconstructions are based, however, on fragmentary evidence that may be subject to the historian's conscious or unconscious manipulation to achieve a "harmonious relationship of parts" or a "logical continuity" that he desires. Historical bias notwithstanding, reconstructions are a necessity inasmuch as they are basic to characterizing such a building. Accurately measured plans and sections are the *sine qua non* of the discipline.

All plans and sections are provided with scales in feet and meters, and north arrows. I had hoped to reproduce most of the plans and sections in the same scale, but I found that doing so would greatly reduce the number that could be included.

The study of the history of architecture requires contact with the monuments themselves. This volume is intended to do no more than provide the neophyte with a chart on which he may plot his voyages, and the initiate with a visual record of what he has seen.

I should like to express my gratitude to the many individuals and institutions who gave aid and advice, particularly to the following: Stanford Anderson, François Bucher, Werner Cahn, Spencer Corbett, Patricia Egan, James Fasanelli, Imre Halasz, H. W. Janson, Richard Krautheimer, Bernard Lemann, William MacDonald, René Millon, Ernest Nash, Joseph Schiffer, and Caroline Shillaber; the Arthur Rotch Memorial Library, Massachusetts Institute of Technology; the Widener Library, Fogg Art Museum Library, Peabody Museum, and the Library of the Graduate School of Design, Harvard University; Avery Architectural Library, Columbia University; and the Institute of Fine Arts, New York University.

HENRY A. MILLON

PART ONE

THE ANCIENT WORLD

LIST OF ILLUSTRATIONS

1. PREHISTORIC AND PRIMITIVE ARCHITECTURE

page 17 Dolmen (tomb), Carnac (Brittany, France). Bronze Age, c. 1500 B.C. (Arch. Phot.)

18 Stonehenge, Salisbury Plain (England). New Stone Age, c. 1800–1400 B.C. (MW, London)

19 Temple, Hal Tarxien (Malta). Bronze Age, exact date uncertain. *View and Plan* (Arch. T.C.I.; C. Ceschi, *Architettura… Malta*, fig. 27)

20 Nuraghe Sant'Antine, Torralba (Sardinia). Bronze Age, exact date uncertain. *Interior, Plan, and Section* (Arch. T.C.I.; Maiuri, fig. 25)

21 Ba Ila Village, Northern Rhodesia (Africa) (Amer. Geog. Soc. of N.Y.)

22 Cliff Dwellings, Mesa Verde (Col.). c. 1100–1300 A.D. (Amer. Mus. of Nat. Hist., N.Y.)

2. EGYPTIAN ARCHITECTURE

23 Step Pyramid of King Zoser, Saqqara. Dynasty III, c. 2650 B.C. (Hirmer)

24 Funerary District of King Zoser, Saqqara. Dynasty III, c. 2650 B.C. *Papyrus Half-Columns and General Plan* (Hirmer; Lange & Hirmer, fig. 1)

25 Pyramids of Mycerinus (c. 2500 B.C.), Chephren (c. 2530 B.C.), and Cheops (c. 2570 B.C.), Giza. Dynasty IV (Hirmer)

26 Pyramid Field, Giza. Dynasty IV. *General Plan* (Reisner, *History of the Giza Necropolis*, II, Cambridge, 1955)

26 Pyramid of Cheops, Giza. Dynasty IV, c. 2570 B.C. *North-South Section* (after L. Borchardt)

26 Group of Mastabas. Dynasty IV. *Reconstruction Drawing* (after A. Badawy)

27 Pyramid of Chephren and Valley Temples, Giza. Dynasty IV, c. 2530 B.C. *Plan* (U. Hölscher, *Das Grabdenkmal des Königs Chephren*, pl. III)

27 Funerary Temple of Mentuhotep, Deir el Bahari. Dynasty XI, c. 2052 B.C. *Reconstruction Drawing* (I. E. S. Edwards, *The Pyramids of Egypt*, fig. 25)

28 Fortress of Uronarti, Uronarti Island (Sudan). Dynasty XII, 1991–1786 B.C. *Southeast Wing and Plan* (Mus. of Fine Arts, Boston; N. F. Wheeler)

29 Festival Hall of Tuthmosis III, Temple of Amun, Karnak. Dynasty XVIII, c. 1470 B.C. *View* (Hirmer)

29 Temple of Amun, Karnak. Dynasty XVIII–XIX. *General Plan* (Chevrier, *Annales*, vol. 36, pl. 1)

30 Pylon of Tuthmosis I, Temple of Amun, Karnak. Dynasty XVIII (Hirmer)

31 Funerary Temple of Queen Hatshepsut, Deir el Bahari. Dynasty XVIII, c. 1480 B.C. *General View* (Hirmer)

32 Funerary Temple of Queen Hatshepsut, Deir el Bahari. Dynasty XVIII, c. 1480 B.C. *Entrance to Chapel of Anubis and Naturium* (Hirmer)

33 Funerary Temple of Queen Hatshepsut, Deir el Bahari. Dynasty XVIII, c. 1480 B.C. *Plan, and Reconstruction Drawing* (Lange & Hirmer, figs. 18 & 19)

34 Official Central Quarter, Tel-el-Amarna. Dynasty XVIII, 1372–1350 B.C. *Plan* (courtesy H. W. Fairman)

34 House of Vizier Nakht, Tel-el-Amarna. Dynasty XVIII, 1372–1350 B.C. *Plan* (*Journ. Egypt. Archaeol.*, 8 (1922), pl. XVII)

35 Houses on Edge of Wady, North Suburb, Tel-el-Amarna. Dynasty XVIII, 1372–1350 B.C. *Reconstruction Drawing* (H. Frankfort & J. D. S. Pendlebury, *The City of Akhenaten*, II, pl. XVII)

page 36 Temple of Amen-Mut-Khonsu, Luxor. Dynasty XVIII, c. 1390 B.C. *Plan* (after N. de Garis Davies)

36 Temple of Amen-Mut-Khonsu, Luxor. Dynasty XVIII, c. 1390 B.C. *Hall of Amenhotep III* (Hirmer)

37 Temple of Amen-Mut-Khonsu, Luxor. Dynasty XVIII–XIX. *Colonnade of Amenhotep III (c. 1390 B.C.), and Court and Pylon of Ramesses II (c. 1260 B.C.)* (Hirmer)

38 Temple of Amun, Karnak. Dynasty XIX, c. 1300 B.C. *Hypostyle Hall of Seti I and Ramesses II* (Kidder Smith)

39 Temple of Horus, Edfu. Ptolemaic period, 237–212 B.C. *Pylon and Court, and Plan* (Hirmer; Lange & Hirmer)

3. ARCHITECTURE OF THE ANCIENT NEAR EAST

40 "White Temple" on Its Ziggurat, Uruk (ancient Erech; present Warka, Iraq). c. 3500–3000 B.C. (courtesy GAI, Baghdad)

41 Gudea with Architectural Plan, from Lagash (Telloh, Iraq). c. 2150 B.C. *The Louvre, Paris* (Thames & Hudson)

41 "White Temple" on Its Ziggurat, Uruk (Warka, Iraq). c. 3500–3000 B.C. *Plan* (H. Frankfort, *Art & Archit. of the Ancient Orient*, fig. 4)

42 Elamite Ziggurat, Dur-Untash (Chugha Zambil, Iran). c. 1250 B.C. (Thames & Hudson)

43 City Plan, including Measurements. c. 1500 B.C. *Redrawn from Clay Tablet found in Nippur (Iraq)* (Thames & Hudson)

43 Khorsabad (Iraq). Late 8th century B.C. *General Plan* (G. Loud, *Khorsabad*, II, Chicago, 1938)

44 Citadel of Sargon II, Khorsabad (Iraq). 742–705 B.C. *Reconstruction Drawing and Plan* Chas. Altman; after V. Place)

45 Ishtar Gate, from Processional Way, Babylon (Iraq). c. 575 B.C. *Reconstruction in State Museums, Berlin* (Photo Museum)

46 Lion Gate, Hattusas (Boghazköy, Turkey). c. 1250 B.C. *Outer Gateway* (Hans Güterbock, Or. Inst.)

47 Persepolis (Iran). 518–460 B.C. *Air View, and Plan* (courtesy Dr. Erich F. Schmidt)

48 Persepolis (Iran). c. 500 B.C. *Staircase to Tripylon* (Or. Inst.)

48 Persepolis (Iran). c. 500 B.C. *Audience Hall of Darius* (Or. Inst.)

49 Palace, Ctesiphon (Iraq). Sassanian, c. 4th century A.D. *Exterior View* (Or. Inst.)

50 Achaemenian Royal Tomb, Naksh-i-Rustam (near Persepolis, Iran). 5th century B.C. *Façade of Rock-Cut Tomb* (Or. Inst.)

50 City Block, Mohenjo-Daro (Pakistan). 2700–1800 B.C. *Plan* (Piggott, *Prehistoric India*, fig. 21)

4. MINOAN AND MYCENAEAN ARCHITECTURE

51 Town of Malthi, Triphylia (Southwest Peloponnesus, Greece). Early and Middle Helladic Periods, c. 2500–1700 B.C. *Plan* (from Valmin, *Swedish Messenia Expedition*, plan IV)

52 Palace of Minos, Knossos (Crete). 1600–1500 B.C. *Grand Staircase, and Portico* (Frantz)

53 Palace of Minos, Knossos (Crete). 1600–1500 B.C. *Plan and Geographical Diagram* (James W. Graham, *The Palaces of Crete*, figs. 2 & 3)

54 "Treasury of Atreus," Mycenae (near Argos, Greece). 1330–1300 B.C. *Interior and Section* (SBB)

55 Palace (1250–1200 B.C.) and South Part of Citadel (1400–1280 B.C.), Tiryns (near Nauplia, Greece). *Plan* (from Kurt Müller, *Tiryns*, vol. III, pl. IV)

56 The Lion Gate, Entrance to Citadel, Mycenae (Greece). 1350–1300 B.C. (Frantz)

5. GREEK ARCHITECTURE

57 "Temple of Poseidon" (c. 460 B.C.) and "Basilica" (c. 550 B.C.), Paestum (Italy) (Kidder Smith)

58 Paestum (Italy). Founded c. 600 B.C. *Air View and Plan* (Fototeca Unione; Maiuri)

page 59 "Basilica," Paestum (Italy). c. 550 B.C. *Southeast Corner, and Plan* (Kidder Smith; R. Koldeney & O. Puchstein, *Die griechischen Tempel... Sicilien*, fig. 71)

60 "Temple of Poseidon," Paestum (Italy). 460 B.C. *Interior and Plan* (Fototeca Unione; Dinsmoor, fig. 36)

61 "Temple of Poseidon," Paestum (Italy). c. 460 B.C. *Restored Section and Corner of Façade* (Alinari; A. Trevor Hodge, *The Woodwork of Greek Roofs*, fig. 2)

62 Treasury of the Siphnians, Sanctuary of Apollo, Delphi. c. 530 B.C. *Reconstruction of Façade in Museum, Delphi* (Stoedtner)

63 Treasury of the Athenians, Sanctuary of Apollo, Delphi. c. 500-485 B.C. (Alinari)

64 Athens. 5th century A.D. *General Plan* (Hill, fig. 1)

64 Agora, Athens. Late 5th century B.C. *Plan* (Scranton, pl. 65)

65 Agora, Athens. 2nd century A.D. *General Plan* (Hill, fig. 2)

65 Agora, Athens. 2nd century A.D. *Plan of Buildings on West Side* (Hill, fig. 8)

66 Acropolis, South Slope, Athens. Late 4th century A.D. *Plan* (Hill, fig. 20)

66 Theater of Dionysus, Lycourgan Theater. Acropolis, Athens. Second half of 4th century B.C. *Plan* (Hill, fig. 17)

67 ICTINUS. Parthenon, Acropolis, Athens. 448-432 B.C. *West Façade* (Frantz)

68 Parthenon, Acropolis, Athens. *Elevation showing "Refinements"* (Balanos, *Les monuments de l'Acropole*, Dépliant no. 2)

68 Parthenon, Acropolis, Athens. 448-432 B.C. *Plan*

69 MNESICLES. Propylaea, Acropolis, Athens. 437-432 B.C. *East Façade* (Frantz)

70 Propylaea (437-432 B.C.) and Temple of Athena Nike (427-424 B.C.), Acropolis, Athens (Frantz)

71 MNESICLES. Propylaea, Acropolis, Athens. 437-432 B.C. *Plan and Section*

72 Erechtheum, Acropolis, Athens. Begun 421 B.C. *West and East Side* (Frantz)

73 Porch of the Maidens, Erechtheum, Acropolis, Athens. Begun 421 B.C. (Hirmer)

73 Erechtheum, Acropolis, Athens. Begun 421 B.C. *Plan of Unrestored Building* (Gorham Stevens and J. M. Paton, *The Erechtheum*, pl. II)

74 Erechtheum, Acropolis, Athens. Begun 421 B.C. *Detail of Moldings, North Porch* (Frantz)

74 *The Acropolis of Athens in 1670* A.D. Pen Drawing, Italian School. *Museo Civico, Bassano (Italy)* (Fondazione Cini)

75 "Theseum" (Temple of Hephaestus), Athens. 449-c. 430 B.C. *View, and Transverse Section of Restored Building* (Frantz; A. Trevor Hodge, *The Woodwork of Greek Roofs*, fig. 4)

76 Olympieion, Athens. c. 170 B.C. *Corinthian Columns, Southeast Corner* (Fototeca Unione)

77 Stoa of Attalos, East Side of Agora, Athens. c. 140 B.C. *View of Exterior as Rebuilt* (Bissantz)

77 Temple of Apollo, Bassae. 450-425 B.C. (Hege)

78 Temple of Apollo, Bassae. 450-425 B.C. *Interior and Plan* (Frantz)

79 Temple of Apollo, Sanctuary at Didyma near Miletus (Palatia, Turkey). Late 4th century B.C. and subsequently (courtesy Prof. Dr. Friedrich Krauss)

80 Temple of Apollo, Sanctuary at Didyma near Miletus (Palatia, Turkey). Begun late 4th century. *Restored Section through Porch and Part of Court* (Wiegand, *Didyma I*, Zeichn. 10)

80 Temple of Apollo, Sanctuary at Didyma near Miletus (Palatia, Turkey). Begun late 4th century. *Restored Plan* (Dinsmoor, fig. 83)

81 City of Miletus (Palatia, Turkey). *General Plan, after 466* B.C. (von Gerkan, *Griech. Stadtanlagen*, pl. 6)

81 City of Miletus. *Plan of Central Public Area, c. 150* B.C. (A. W. Lawrence, fig. 143)

82 Olynthus (Macedonia). 430-348 B.C. *Plan of City Blocks, and Restored Plan of House* (Robinson, *Excavations at Olynthus*, XII, pl. 1; Lawrence, fig. 137)

83 Houses E and F, Section II, Delos. *Plan (Exploration Archéologique de Delos*, VIII, pls. III & IV)

83 Ekklesiasterion (Council House?), Priene (Menderes, Turkey). c. 200 B.C. *Restored Interior, and Plan* (Lawrence, fig. 161)

84 Altar of Zeus, Pergamum (Bergama, Turkey). Begun 180-170 B.C. *Plan, and Reconstruction of West Front in State Museums, Berlin* (after J. Schrammen; photo Museum)

84 Tholos, Sanctuary of Asclepius, Epidaurus. c. 360 B.C. *Plan* (Cavvadias, *Fouilles d'Epidaure I*, pl. IV)

page 85 Theater, Sanctuary of Asclepius, Epidaurus. c. 350 B.C. *View and Plan* (Frantz; Pickard-Cambridge, *Theatre of Dionysus in Athens*, fig. 70)

6. ETRUSCAN ARCHITECTURE

86 City of Marzabotto, southwest of Bologna. Late 6th–early 5th centuries B.C. *Plan* (Maiuri, fig. 63)

87 Porta Augusta (City Gate), Perugia. 2nd century B.C. *Exterior Façade* (Anderson)

88 Burial Chamber, "Tomb of the Reliefs," Cerveteri. 4th century B.C. *View Showing Stucco Reliefs* (Alterocca)

7. ROMAN ARCHITECTURE

89 City of Timgad (Algeria). 100–117 A.D. *Plan* (Boethius, *Golden House*, fig. 22)

90 Forum Romanum, Rome. 1st century B.C. to 4th century A.D. *Plan* (T.C.I.)

91 Imperial Forums, Rome. 1st to 3rd century A.D. *Plan, and Reconstruction Model* (Fototeca Unione)

92 Forum of Trajan, Rome. c. 113–17 A.D. *Plan of Basilica Ulpia* (courtesy Prof. William MacDonald, Yale University)

92 Forum of Trajan, Rome. c. 113–17 A.D. *View of Mercati (Market Buildings)* (Fototeca Unione)

93 Maison Carrée, Nîmes (France). Completed 16 B.C. (Schmidt-Glassner)

94 Temple of the Sibyl, Tivoli. Early 1st century B.C. *View and Plan* (Kidder Smith)

95 Theater of Marcellus, Rome. 1st century B.C. *Exterior and Plan* (Fototeca Unione)

96 Colosseum, Rome. 72–80 A.D. *Air View, and Exterior* (Fotocielo; Fototeca Unione)

97 Colosseum, Rome. 72–80 A.D. *Plan and Section* (T.C.I.)

98 Temple of Bacchus, Baalbek (Lebanon). 2nd century A.D. *Interior of Cella* (Kidder Smith)

99 Temple of Venus, Baalbek (Lebanon). 3rd century A.D. *Exterior and Plan* (SBB; Wiegand, *Baalbek*, II, fig. 130)

100 Temple Enclosure, Baalbek (Lebanon). 1st to 2nd century A.D. *Reconstruction Drawing, and Plan* (Collart and Coupel, *L'autel… Baalbek*, Paris, 1951; Wiegand, *Baalbek*, I, pl. 14)

101 GIOVANNI PAOLO PANINI. *The Interior of the Pantheon*. c. 1750 A.D. *National Gallery of Art, Washington, D.C. (Kress Collection)*

102 Pantheon, Rome. c. 118–25 A.D. *Façade* (Fototeca Unione)

103 Pantheon, Rome. c. 118–25 A.D. *Structural Diagram* (after L. Beltrami)

104 Pantheon, Rome. c. 118–25 A.D. *Plan, and Reconstruction Model* (Sopr. Mon. Lazio; Fototeca Unione)

105 Basilica, Leptis Magna (Libya). Early 3rd century A.D. *Plan and Interior* (GAI, Rome)

106 Baths of Caracalla, Rome. 212–23 A.D. *Plan* (Amer. Acad., Rome)

107 Baths of Caracalla, Rome. 212–23 A.D. *Reconstruction Rendering*

107 Baths of Caracalla, Rome. 212–23 A.D. *Air View* (Fototeca Unione)

108 Basilica of Constantine, Rome. c. 310–20 A.D. *View and Plan* (Kidder Smith)

109 Monumental Arch, Susa. c. 8 B.C. (Fototeca Unione)

109 Arch of Constantine, Rome. Early 4th century A.D. (Anderson)

110 House of the Vettii, Pompeii. c. 50 A.D. *Peristyle* (Alinari)

110 House of Neptune and Amphitrite, Herculaneum. 1st century B.C. *Atrium* (Alinari)

111 Fragment of *Forma Urbis* (Plan of Rome). c. 200 A.D. *Museo Comune, Rome*

111 *Architectural View*, from a villa at Boscoreale. 1st century B.C. *The Metropolitan Museum of Art, New York (Rogers Fund, 1903)*

112 Apartment House (House of Diana), Ostia. 2nd century A.D. *Street Façade and Plan* (Fototeca Unione)

113 Piazza d'Oro, Hadrian's Villa, Tivoli. 125–35 A.D. *Plan* (Fototeca Unione)

114 Circular Casino, Hadrian's Villa, Tivoli. 125–35 A.D. *View and Plan* (Fototeca Unione)

115 Palace of Diocletian, Split (Yugoslavia). c. 300 A.D. *Plan (engraved 1764 by Robert Adam), and Ceremonial Court* (courtesy State Tourist Office of Yugoslavia, N. Y.)

page 116 Mausoleum, Palace of Diocletian, Split (Yugoslavia). c. 300 A.D. *Interior View* (engraving from Robert Adam, *Ruins of the Palace of the Emperor Diocletian*, 1764; courtesy The Metropolitan Museum of Art, N. Y., Beattie Collection, 1941)

117 Palace of Diocletian, Split (Yugoslavia). c. 300 A.D. *Section of Mausoleum, and East Gate of Palace* (Fototeca Unione; Marburg)

118 Pont du Gard (viaduct and aqueduct), near Nîmes (France). Early 1st century A.D. (Roubier)

119 Market Gate, Miletus (Palatia, Turkey). c. 160 A.D. *Reconstruction in State Museums, Berlin*

120 Porta Nigra (fortified city gate), Trier (Germany). Early 4th century A.D. *Façade* (SBB)

120 Harbor, Ostia. Largely 1st and 2nd century A.D. *Plan* (R. Meiggs, *Roman Ostia*, fig. 6)

8. EARLY CHRISTIAN ARCHITECTURE

121 S. Costanza, Rome. c. 350. *Interior* (GAI, Rome)

122 S. Costanza, Rome. c. 350. *Plan and Section* (courtesy Dr. Michael Stettler, Bern)

123 Church of the Nativity, Bethlehem (Jordan). Begun c. 326. *Plan* (after J. W. Crowfoot)

124 S. Stefano Rotondo, Rome. 468–83. *Interior and Plan* (Alinari; courtesy Spencer Corbett)

125 Church, Qalb Lauzeh (Syria). c. 500. *Exterior and Plan* (courtesy Prof. H. C. Butler, Princeton University; de Vogüé, *La Syrie Centrale)*

126 Basilica, Trier (Germany). Early 4th century. *Exterior* (Landesmuseum, Trier)

127 Old St. Peter's, Vatican City (Rome). c. 333. *Interior, fresco on nave wall of S. Martino ai Monti, Rome* (Alinari)

128 Old St. Peter's, Vatican City (Rome). c. 333. *Plan and Section* (courtesy Prof. Alfred Frazer, Vassar College)

129 S. Maria Maggiore, Rome. 432–40. *Interior* (Anderson)

129 Mausoleum of Galla Placidia, Ravenna (Italy). c. 450. *Exterior* (Hirmer)

130 S. Apollinare Nuovo, Ravenna (Italy). c. 520. *Interior* (Anderson)

130 S. Apollinare in Classe (near Ravenna, Italy). c. 530–49. *Air View* (Fotocielo)

131 S. Apollinare in Classe (near Ravenna, Italy). c. 530–49. *Interior and Plan* (Anderson; F. de Dartein, *Étude sur l'architecture lombarde*, pl. 3)

132 Baptistery of the Orthodox, Ravenna (Italy). First half of 5th century. *Interior and Plan* (Alinari; courtesy Dr. Spiro K. Kostof, Yale University)

133 S. Lorenzo Maggiore, Milan (Italy). c. 480. *Plan* (A. Calderini, *La Basilica... Milano)*

133 Baptistery of the Orthodox, Ravenna (Italy). First half of 5th century. *Exterior* (Alinari)

9. BYZANTINE ARCHITECTURE

134 S. Vitale, Ravenna (Italy). 526–47. *Interior* (Ed. E.S.)

135 S. Vitale, Ravenna (Italy). 526–47. *Exterior, Plan, and Section* (Kidder Smith; *L'Architettura II*, p. 522)

136 SS. Sergius and Bacchus, Istanbul (Turkey). c. 527. *Interior* (Dr. Helmut Hell)

137 SS. Sergius and Bacchus, Istanbul (Turkey). c. 527. *Plan and Section* (J. Ebersolt, *Les Églises de Constantinople)*

138 ANTHEMIUS OF TRALLES and ISIDORUS OF MILETUS. Hagia Sophia, Istanbul (Turkey). 532–37. *Exterior* (Kidder Smith)

139 ANTHEMIUS OF TRALLES and ISIDORUS OF MILETUS. Hagia Sophia, Istanbul (Turkey). 532–37. *Plan and Section* (E. H. Swift, *Hagia Sophia)*

140 ANTHEMIUS OF TRALLES and ISIDORUS OF MILETUS. Hagia Sophia, Istanbul (Turkey). 532–37. *Interior* (Hirmer)

141 ANTHEMIUS OF TRALLES and ISIDORUS OF MILETUS. Hagia Sophia, Istanbul (Turkey). 532–37. *Interior* (courtesy Prof. William MacDonald, Yale University)

142 Churches of St. Luke of Stiris and of the Virgin, Monastery of Hosios Loukas, Phocis (Greece). Early 11th century. *Exterior* (Frantz)

143 Church of St. Luke of Stiris, Monastery of Hosios Loukas, Phocis (Greece). Early 11th century. *Interior and Plan* (Frantz; C. Diehl, *L'Église... Phocide*, opp. p. 72)

144 Cathedral of St. Basil, Moscow (Russia). 1554–60. *Exterior* (Sibbelee)

144 Church of the Dormition, Vladimir (Russia). 1158–61; rebuilt 1185–89. *Exterior* (Tass)

THE ANCIENT WORLD

1. Prehistoric and Primitive Architecture

Dolmen (tomb), Carnac (Brittany, France).
Bronze Age, c. 1500 B.C.

Stonehenge, Salisbury Plain (England). New Stone Age, c. 1800–1400 B.C.
Outer diameter 106′; tallest stones 13 1/2′ above ground.
Air View toward southeast, and View between Outer Circles

Temple, Hal Tarxien (Malta).
Bronze Age, exact date uncertain.
View of Entrance, and Plan

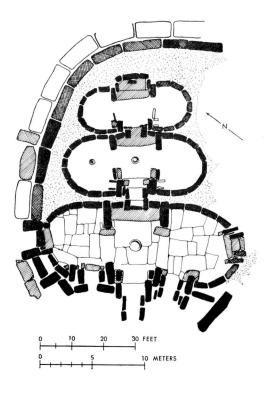

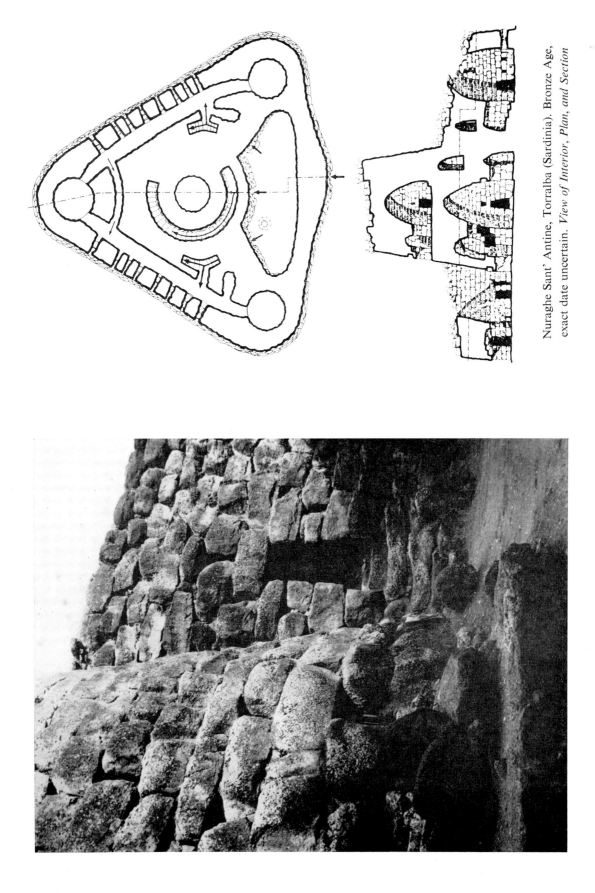

Nuraghe Sant' Antine, Torralba (Sardinia). Bronze Age, exact date uncertain. *View of Interior, Plan, and Section*

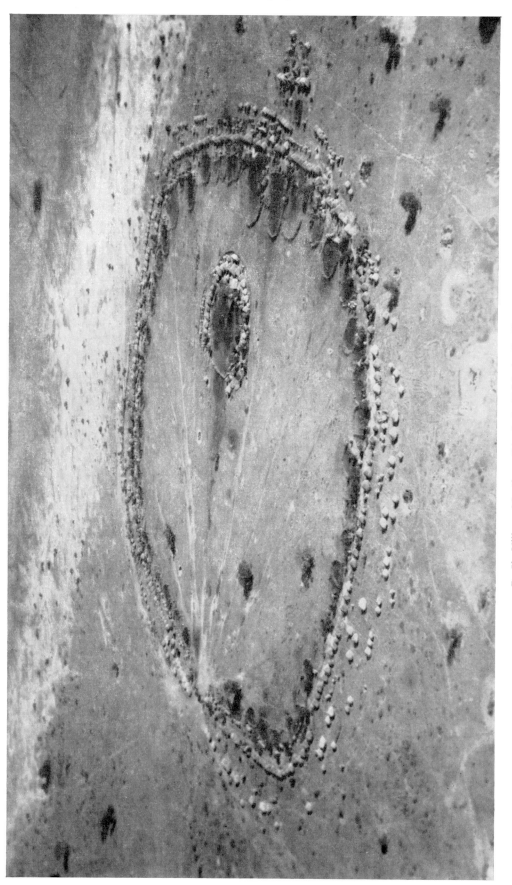

Ba Ila Village, Northern Rhodesia (Africa). *Air View*

Cliff Dwellings, Mesa Verde (Colorado). c. 1100–1300 A.D.

THE ANCIENT WORLD

2. Egyptian Architecture

ALL LOCATIONS ARE IN EGYPT UNLESS OTHERWISE NOTED

Step Pyramid of King Zoser, Saqqara. Dynasty III,
c. 2650 B.C. *View from the south*

Funerary District of King Zoser, Saqqara. Dynasty III, c. 2650 B.C.
Papyrus Half-Columns on East Façade of North Palace, and General Plan of District

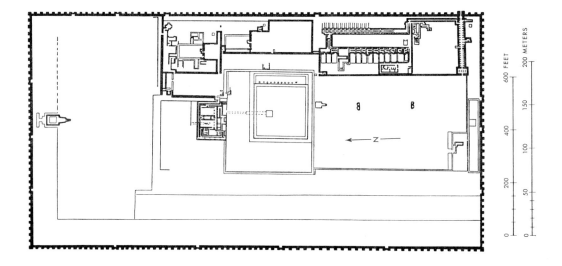

Pyramids of Mycerinus (left, c. 2500 B.C.), Chephren (center, c. 2530 B.C.), and Cheops (right, c. 2570 B.C.), Giza. Dynasty IV. *View from the south*

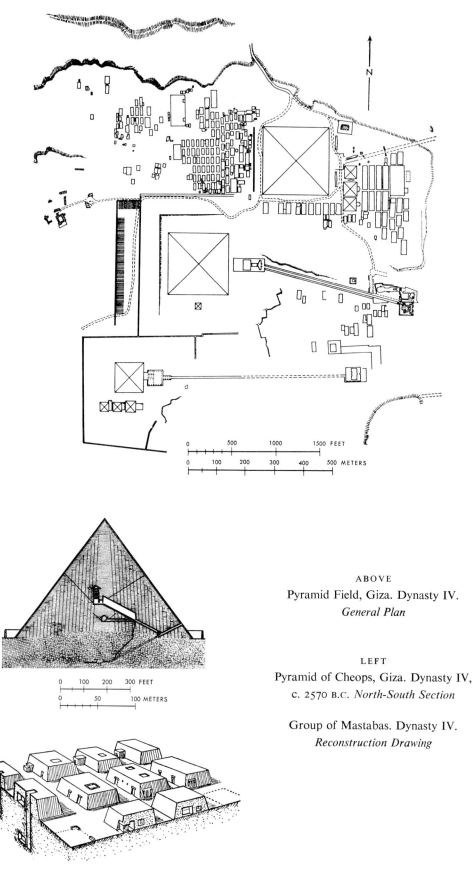

ABOVE
Pyramid Field, Giza. Dynasty IV.
General Plan

LEFT
Pyramid of Cheops, Giza. Dynasty IV,
c. 2570 B.C. *North-South Section*

Group of Mastabas. Dynasty IV.
Reconstruction Drawing

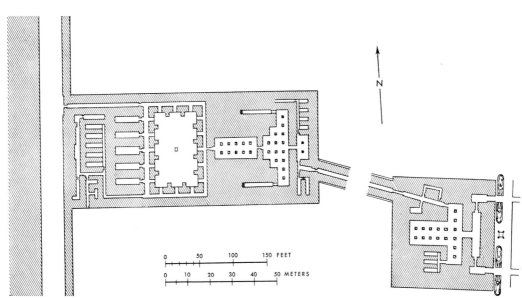

Pyramid of Chephren and Valley Temples, Giza. Dynasty IV,
c. 2530 B.C. *Plan*

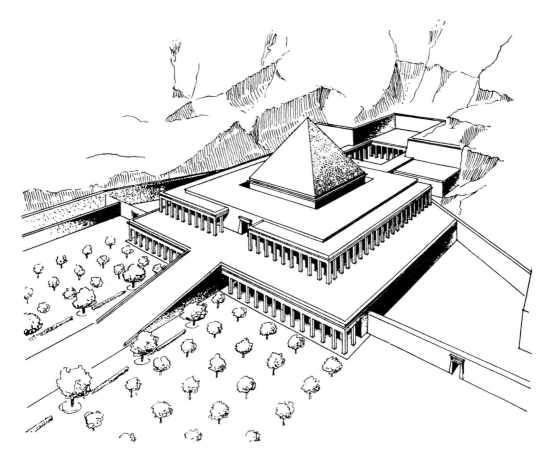

Funerary Temple of Mentuhotep, Deir el Bahari. Dynasty XI,
c. 2052 B.C. *Reconstruction Drawing*

Fortress of Uronarti, Uronarti Island (above 2nd Cataract of the Nile, Sudan).
Dynasty XII, 1991–1786 B.C. *View of Southeast Wing, and General Plan*

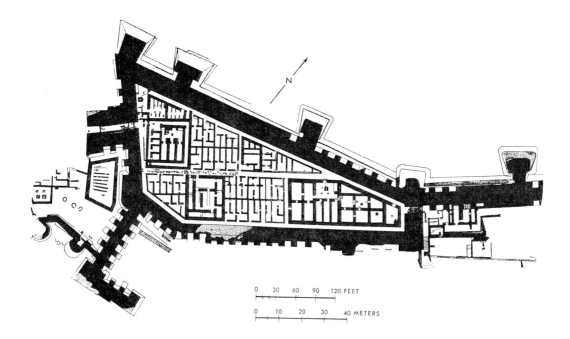

N

| 0 | 30 | 60 | 90 | 120 FEET |

| 0 | 10 | 20 | 30 | 40 METERS |

Festival Hall of Tuthmosis III, Temple of Amun, Karnak.
Dynasty XVIII, c. 1470 B.C. *View from southwest (a on Plan)*

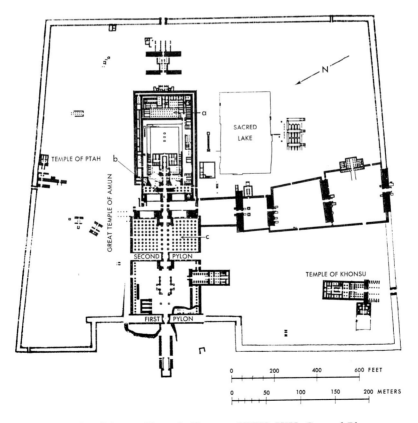

Temple of Amun, Karnak. Dynasty XVIII–XIX. *General Plan*

Pylon of Tuthmosis I, Temple of Amun, Karnak. Dynasty XVIII.
View toward the east: left, Obelisk of Tuthmosis I (1530–1520 B.C.*);*
right, Obelisk of Queen Hatshepsut (1511–1480 B.C.*);* b *on Plan, p. 29*

Funerary Temple of Queen Hatshepsut, Deir el Bahari. Dynasty XVIII, c. 1480 B.C.

General View from northwest

Funerary Temple of Queen Hatshepsut, Deir el Bahari. Dynasty XVIII, c. 1480 B.C.
Entrance to Chapel of Anubis and Naturium

Funerary Temple of Queen Hatshepsut,
Deir el Bahari. Dynasty XVIII, c. 1480 B.C.
*Plan, and Reconstruction Drawing
from northeast (Funerary Temple
of Mentuhotep in Background)*

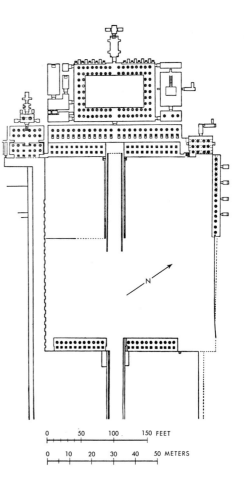

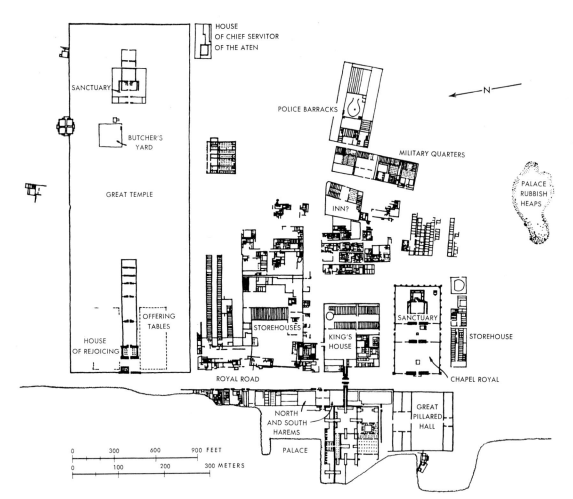

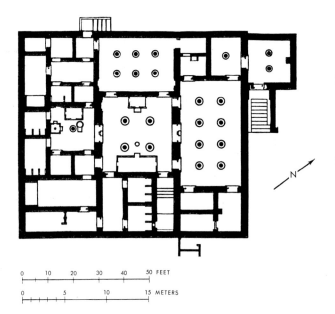

SANCTUARY

HOUSE
OF CHIEF SERVITOR
OF THE ATEN

BUTCHER'S
YARD

GREAT TEMPLE

POLICE BARRACKS

MILITARY QUARTERS

N

PALACE
RUBBISH
HEAPS

INN?

OFFERING
TABLES

HOUSE
OF REJOICING

STOREHOUSES

KING'S
HOUSE

SANCTUARY

STOREHOUSE

CHAPEL ROYAL

ROYAL ROAD

NORTH
AND SOUTH
HAREMS

GREAT
PILLARED
HALL

PALACE

0   300   600   900 FEET

0   100   200   300 METERS

ABOVE
Official Central Quarter,
Tel-el-Amarna. Dynasty XVIII,
1372–1350 B.C. *Plan*

LEFT
House of Vizier Nakht,
Tel-el-Amarna. Dynasty XVIII,
1372–1350 B.C. *Plan*

N

0   10   20   30   40   50 FEET

0   5   10   15 METERS

Houses on Edge of Wady (river bed), North Suburb, Tel-el-Amarna.
Dynasty XVIII, 1372–1350 B.C. *Reconstruction Drawing*

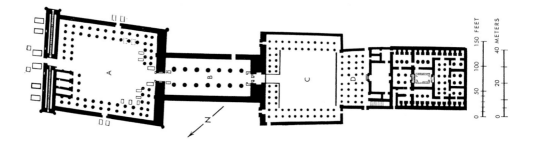

Temple of Amen-Mut-Khonsu, Luxor. Dynasty XVIII, c. 1390 B.C.
Plan, and Hall of Amenhotep III from the west (d on Plan)

Temple of Amen-Mut-Khonsu, Luxor. Dynasty XVIII–XIX. *View toward the east: Colonnade of Amenhotep III (c. 1390 B.C.; b on Plan), and Court and Pylon of Ramesses II (c. 1260 B.C.; a on Plan)*

Temple of Amun, Karnak. Dynasty XIX, c. 1300 B.C.
Hypostyle Hall of Seti I and Ramesses II (c on Plan, p. 29)

Temple of Horus, Edfu. Ptolemaic Period, 237–212 B.C. *Pylon and Court from northeast, and Plan*

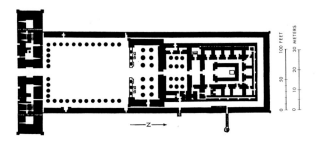

THE ANCIENT WORLD

3. *Architecture of the Ancient Near East*

"White Temple" on Its Ziggurat, Uruk (ancient Erech; present Warka, Iraq).
c. 3500–3000 B.C. *View from the west*

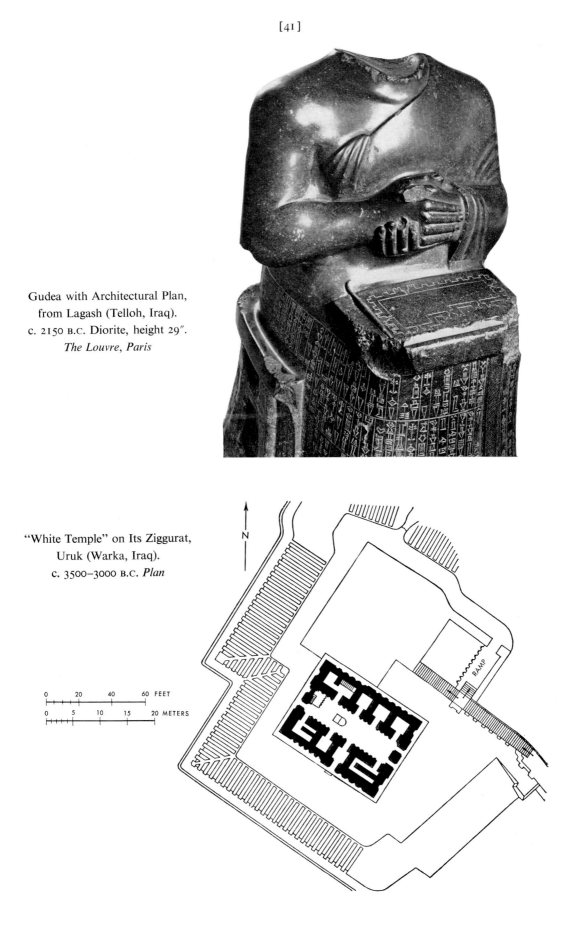

Gudea with Architectural Plan,
from Lagash (Telloh, Iraq).
c. 2150 B.C. Diorite, height 29″.
The Louvre, Paris

"White Temple" on Its Ziggurat,
Uruk (Warka, Iraq).
c. 3500–3000 B.C. *Plan*

Elamite Ziggurat, Dur-Untash (Chugha Zambil, Iran). c. 1250 B.C.

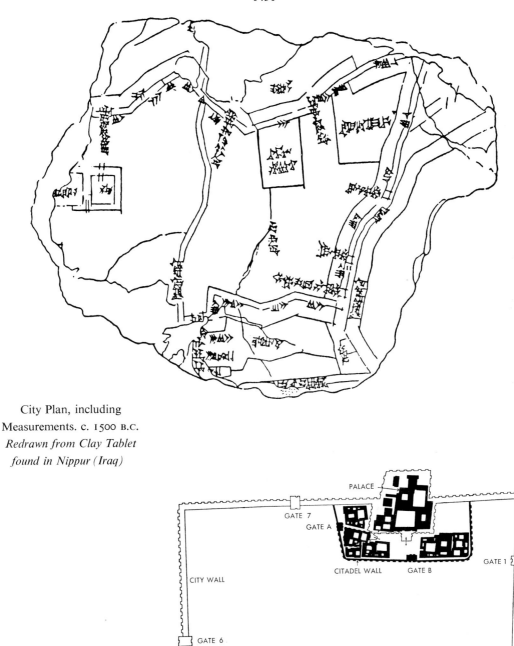

City Plan, including
Measurements. c. 1500 B.C.
*Redrawn from Clay Tablet
found in Nippur (Iraq)*

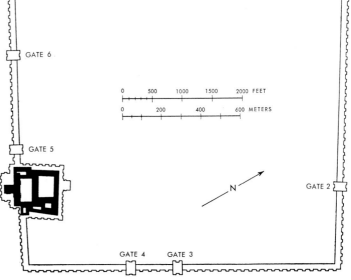

Khorsabad (Iraq).
Late 8th century B.C.
General Plan

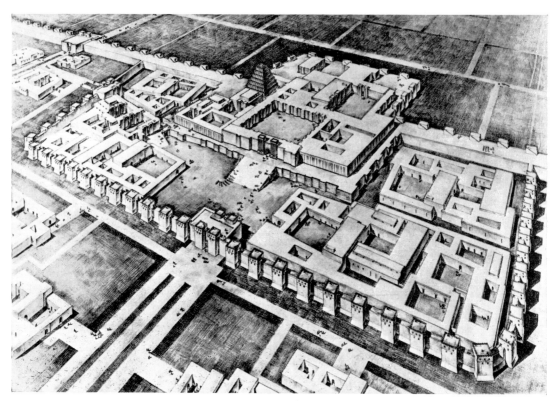

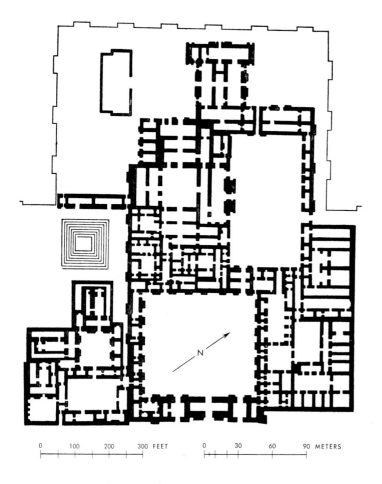

Citadel of Sargon II,
Khorsabad (Iraq). 742–705 B.C.
*Reconstruction Drawing
and Plan*

0   100   200   300 FEET   0   30   60   90 METERS

Ishtar Gate, from Processional Way, Babylon (Iraq). c. 575 B.C.
Reconstruction in State Museums, Berlin

Lion Gate, Hattusas (Boghazköy, Turkey). c. 1250 B.C. *Outer Gateway, from southwest*

Persepolis (Iran). 518–460 B.C. *Air View from southwest, and Plan*

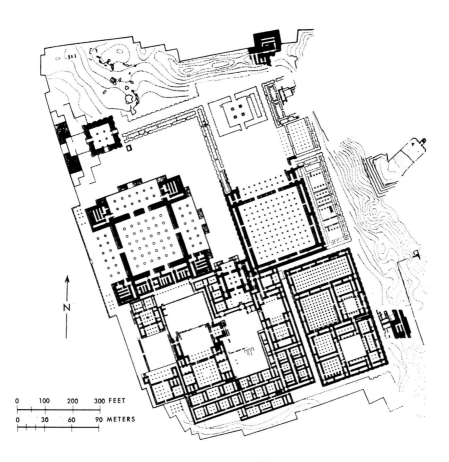

Persepolis (Iran). c. 500 B.C. *Staircase to Tripylon, from the north*

Persepolis (Iran). c. 500 B.C. *Audience Hall of Darius, from the west*

Palace, Ctesiphon (Iraq). Sassanian, c. 4th century A.D. *Exterior View from the north*

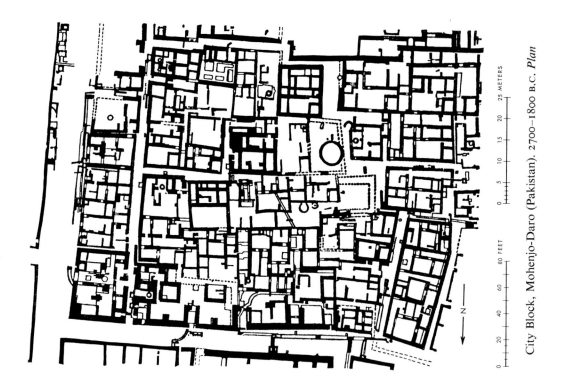

City Block, Mohenjo-Daro (Pakistan). 2700–1800 B.C. *Plan*

Achaemenian Royal Tomb, Naksh-i-Rustam (near Persepolis, Iran).
5th century B.C. *Façade of Rock-Cut Tomb*

THE ANCIENT WORLD

4. Minoan and Mycenaean Architecture

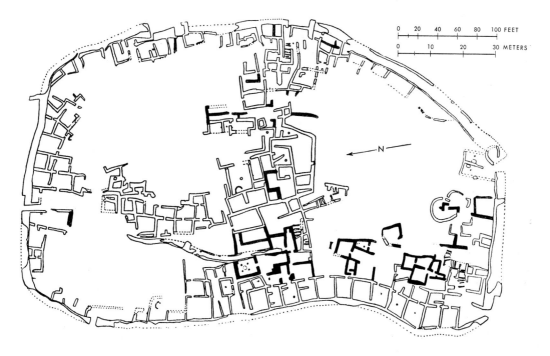

Town of Malthi, Triphylia (Southwest Peloponnesus, Greece).
Early and Middle Helladic Periods c. 2500–1700 B.C. *Plan (Late Helladic
additions in solid black)*

Palace of Minos,
Knossos (Crete).
1600–1500 B.C.
*Grand Staircase
(*a *on Plan),
and Portico with
Stucco Relief of a Bull,
from North Entrance
(*b *on Plan)*

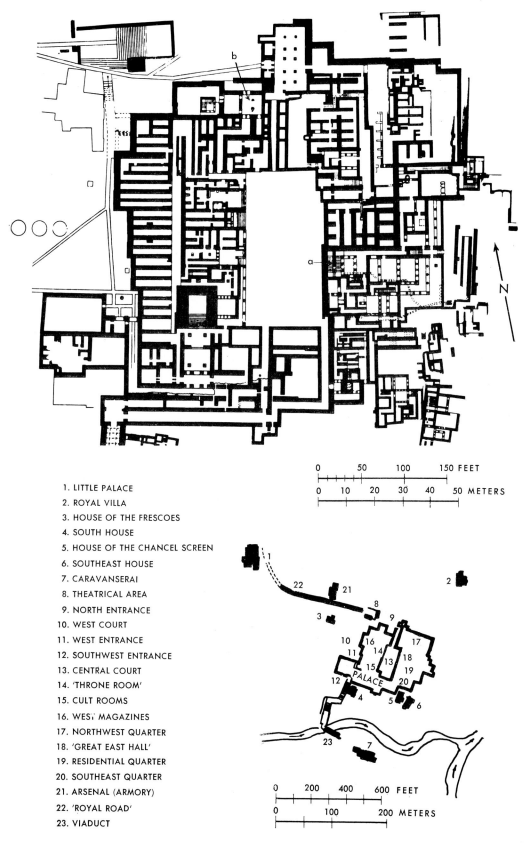

0   50   100   150 FEET

0   10   20   30   40   50 METERS

1. LITTLE PALACE
2. ROYAL VILLA
3. HOUSE OF THE FRESCOES
4. SOUTH HOUSE
5. HOUSE OF THE CHANCEL SCREEN
6. SOUTHEAST HOUSE
7. CARAVANSERAI
8. THEATRICAL AREA
9. NORTH ENTRANCE
10. WEST COURT
11. WEST ENTRANCE
12. SOUTHWEST ENTRANCE
13. CENTRAL COURT
14. 'THRONE ROOM'
15. CULT ROOMS
16. WEST MAGAZINES
17. NORTHWEST QUARTER
18. 'GREAT EAST HALL'
19. RESIDENTIAL QUARTER
20. SOUTHEAST QUARTER
21. ARSENAL (ARMORY)
22. 'ROYAL ROAD'
23. VIADUCT

0   200   400   600 FEET

0   100   200 METERS

Palace of Minos, Knossos (Crete). 1600–1500 B.C. *Plan and Geographical Diagram with Key*

"Treasury of Atreus," Tholos (Beehive) Tomb, Mycenae (near Argos, Greece).
1330–1300 B.C. *Interior and Transverse Section*

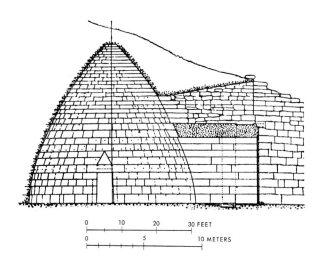

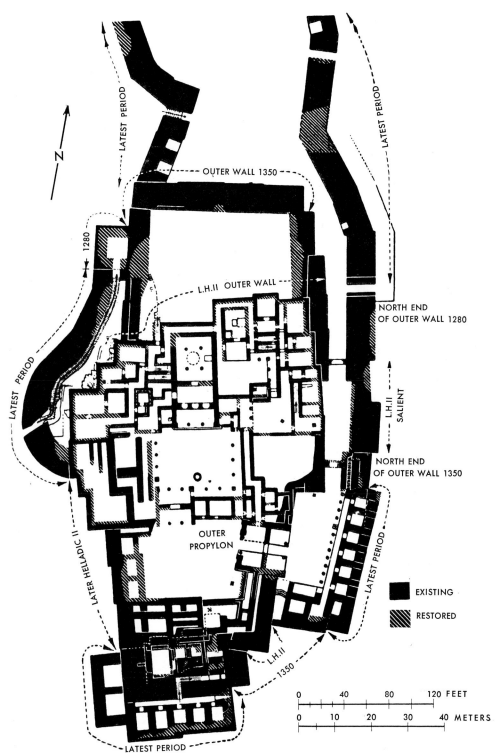

Palace (1250–1200 B.C.) and South Part of Citadel (1400–1280 B.C.),
Tiryns (near Nauplia, Greece). *Plan*

The Lion Gate, Entrance to Citadel, Mycenae (Greece). 1350–1300 B.C.
View from the north

THE ANCIENT WORLD

5. *Greek Architecture*

ALL LOCATIONS ARE IN GREECE UNLESS OTHERWISE NOTED

"Temple of Poseidon" (left, c. 460 B.C.) and "Basilica" (right, c. 550 B.C.),
Paestum (Italy). *View from northeast*

Paestum (Italy). Founded c. 600 B.C. *Air View and Plan*

"Basilica," Paestum (Italy). c. 550 B.C.
Southeast Corner, and Plan

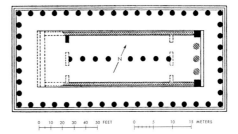

0 10 20 30 40 50 FEET   0   5   10   15 METERS

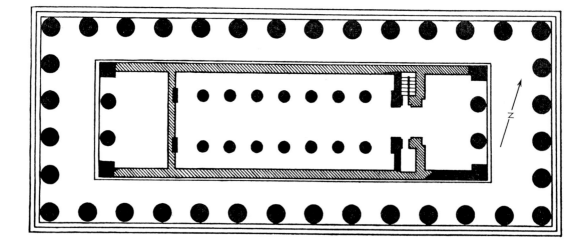

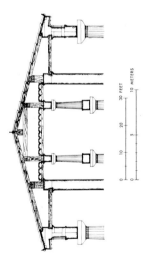

"Temple of Poseidon," Paestum (Italy). c. 460 B.C.
Plan (same scale as Section), and View of Interior toward the south

ABOVE AND RIGHT

"Temple of Poseidon," Paestum (Italy). c. 460 B.C.
Transverse Section (restored), and Corner of Façade

Treasury of the Siphnians, Sanctuary of Apollo, Delphi.
C. 530 B.C. *Reconstruction of Façade in Museum, Delphi*

Treasury of the Athenians, Sanctuary of Apollo, Delphi.
c. 500–485 B.C. *View from northwest*

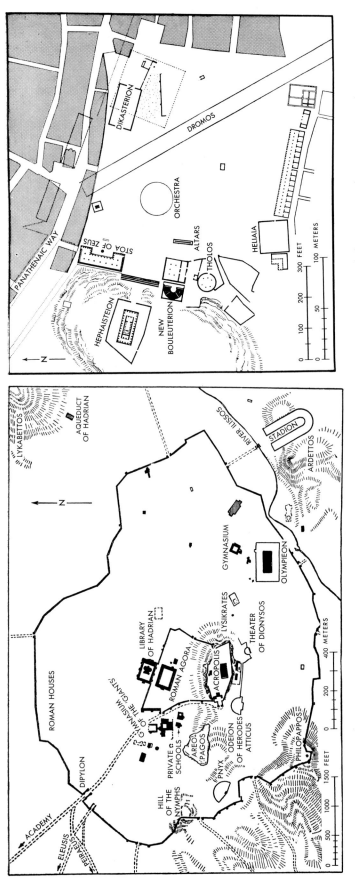

Agora, Athens. Late 5th century B.C. *Plan*

BELOW
Agora, Athens. 2nd century A.D. *Plan of Buildings on West Side*

Athens. 5th century A.D. *General Plan including Greek and Roman Sites*

BELOW
Agora, Athens. 2nd century A.D. *General Plan including Environs*

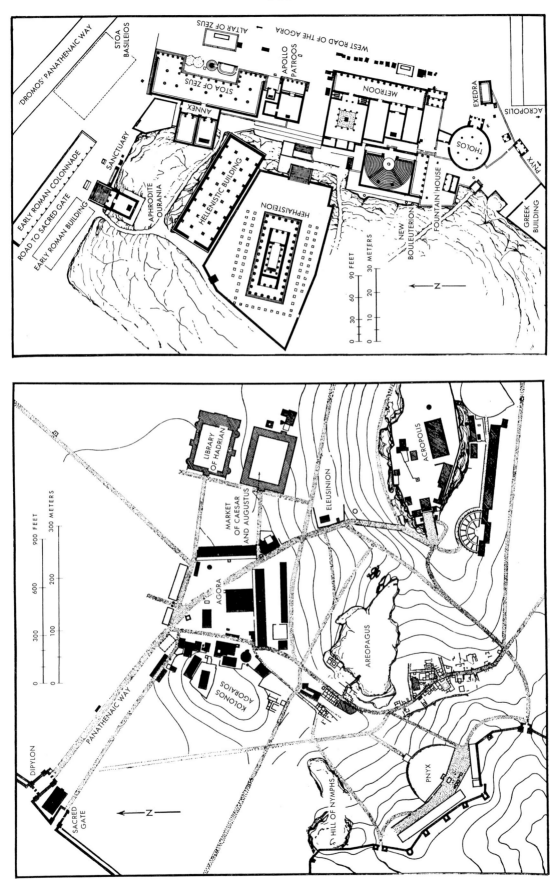

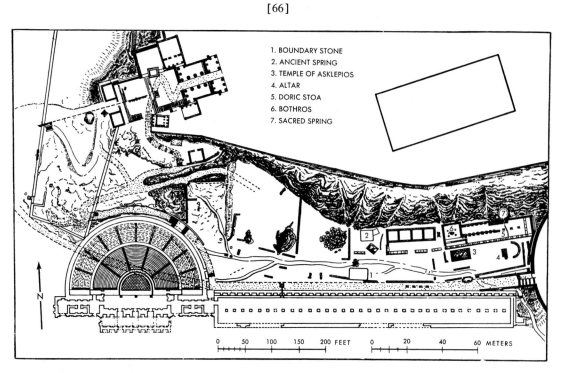

1. BOUNDARY STONE
2. ANCIENT SPRING
3. TEMPLE OF ASKLEPIOS
4. ALTAR
5. DORIC STOA
6. BOTHROS
7. SACRED SPRING

Acropolis, South Slope, Athens. Late 4th century A.D. *Plan*

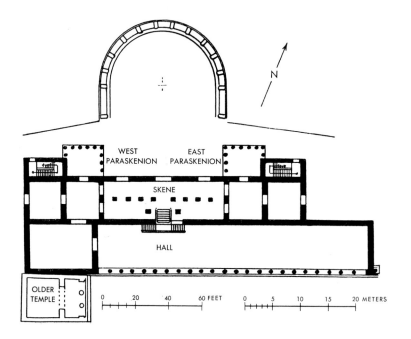

Theater of Dionysus, Lycourgan Theater. Acropolis, Athens.
Second half of 4th century B.C. *Plan*

ICTINUS. Parthenon, Acropolis, Athens. 448–432 B.C. *View of West Façade*

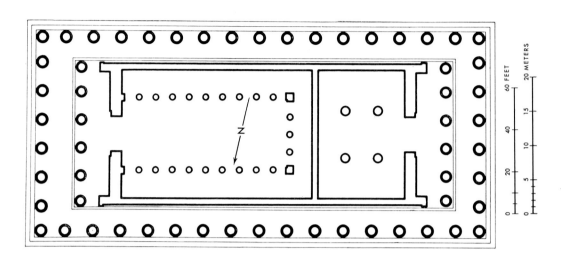

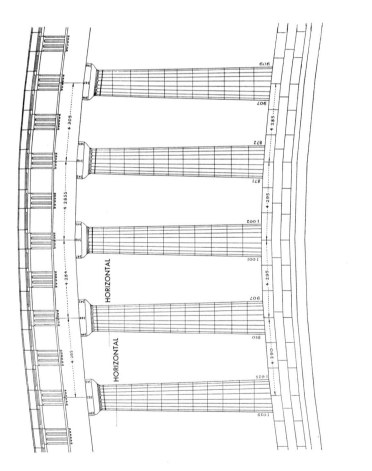

ABOVE

Parthenon, Acropolis, Athens. *Elevation showing "Refinements"*

RIGHT

Parthenon, Acropolis, Athens. 448–432 B.C. *Plan*

MNESICLES. Propylaea, Acropolis, Athens. 437–432 B.C. *View of East Façade*

Propylaea (437–432 B.C.) and Temple of Athena Nike (427–424 B.C.),
Acropolis, Athens. *View from the west*

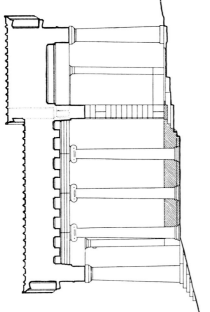

MNESICLES. Propylaea, Acropolis, Athens. 437–432 B.C.
Plan and Longitudinal Section

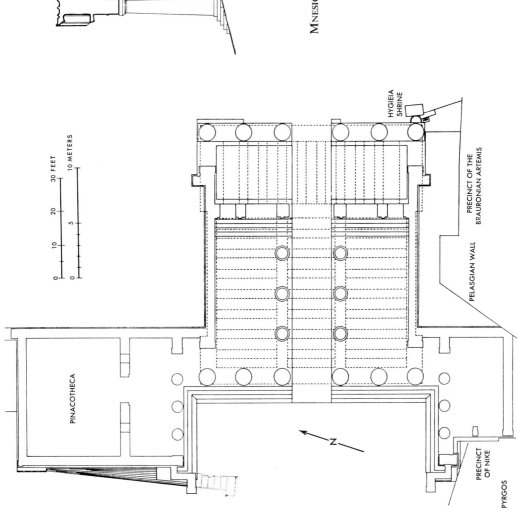

Erechtheum, Acropolis, Athens. Begun 421 B.C. *View from the west (above),*
and from the east (below)

Porch of the Maidens,
Erechtheum, Acropolis,
Athens. Begun 421 B.C.
View from the south

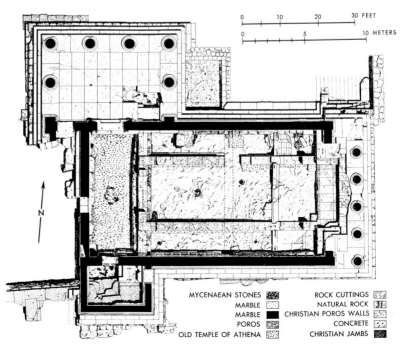

Erechtheum, Acropolis,
Athens. Begun 421 B.C.
Plan of Unrestored Building

MYCENAEAN STONES	ROCK CUTTINGS
MARBLE	NATURAL ROCK
MARBLE	CHRISTIAN POROS WALLS
POROS	CONCRETE
OLD TEMPLE OF ATHENA	CHRISTIAN JAMBS

0   10   20   30 FEET

0   5   10 METERS

N

Erechtheum, Acropolis,
Athens. Begun 421 B.C.
Detail of Moldings,
North Porch

The Acropolis of Athens in 1670 A.D. Pen Drawing,
Italian School. *Museo Civico, Bassano (Italy)*

"Theseum" (Temple of Hephaestus), Athens. Begun 449 B.C.,
construction interrupted, resumed c. 430 B.C. with altered design.
View from southwest, and Transverse Section of Restored Building

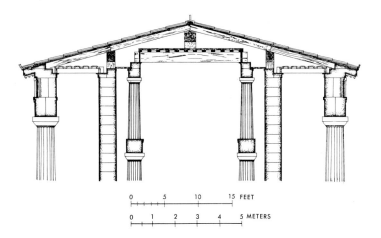

0   5   10   15 FEET

0 1 2 3 4 5 METERS

Olympieion, Athens. c. 170 B.C. *Corinthian Columns, Southeast Corner*

Stoa of Attalos, East Side of Agora, Athens. c. 140 B.C.
View of Exterior as Rebuilt

Temple of Apollo, Bassae. 450–425 B.C. *View from northeast*

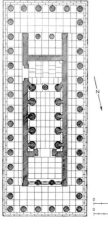

Temple of Apollo, Bassae. 450–425 B.C.
View of Interior, and Plan

Temple of Apollo, Sanctuary at Didyma near Miletus (Palatia, Turkey).
Late 4th century B.C. and subsequently. *View into Porch*

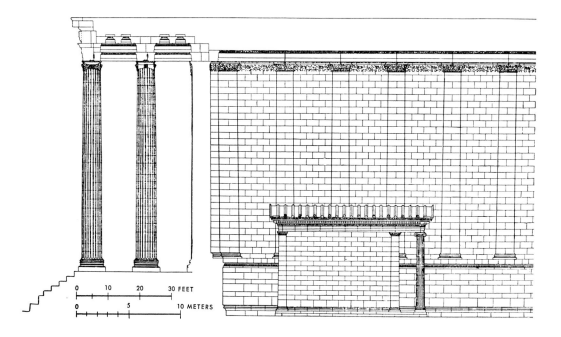

Temple of Apollo, Sanctuary at Didyma near Miletus (Palatia, Turkey). Begun late 4th century B.C.
Longitudinal Section (restored) through Porch and Part of Court

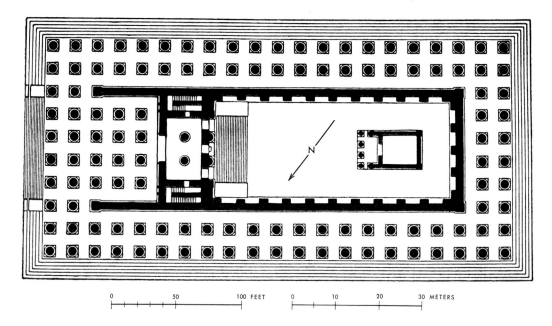

Temple of Apollo, Sanctuary at Didyma near Miletus (Palatia, Turkey).
Begun late 4th century B.C. *Restored Plan*

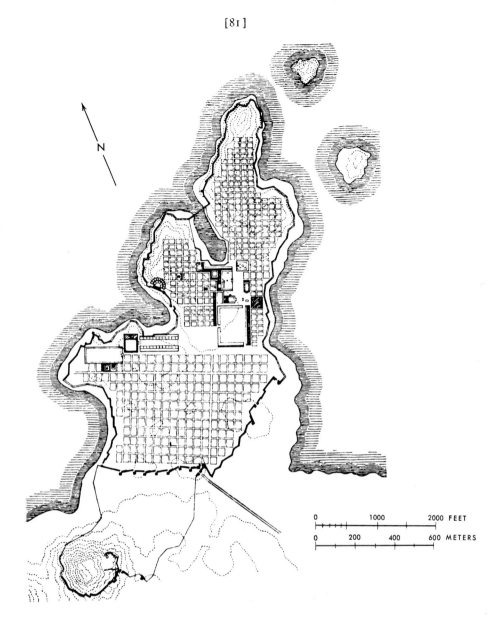

ABOVE
City of Miletus (Palatia, Turkey).
General Plan, after 466 B.C.

RIGHT
City of Miletus (Palatia, Turkey).
Plan of Central Public Area,
c. 150 B.C.

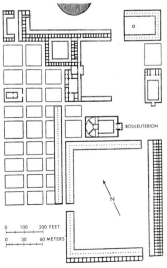

BOULEUTERION

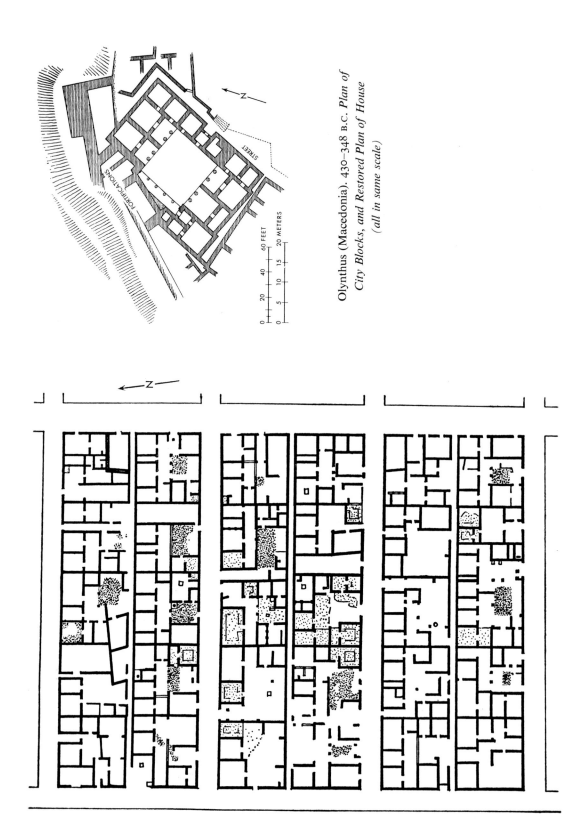

Olynthus (Macedonia). 430–348 B.C. *Plan of
City Blocks, and Restored Plan of House
(all in same scale)*

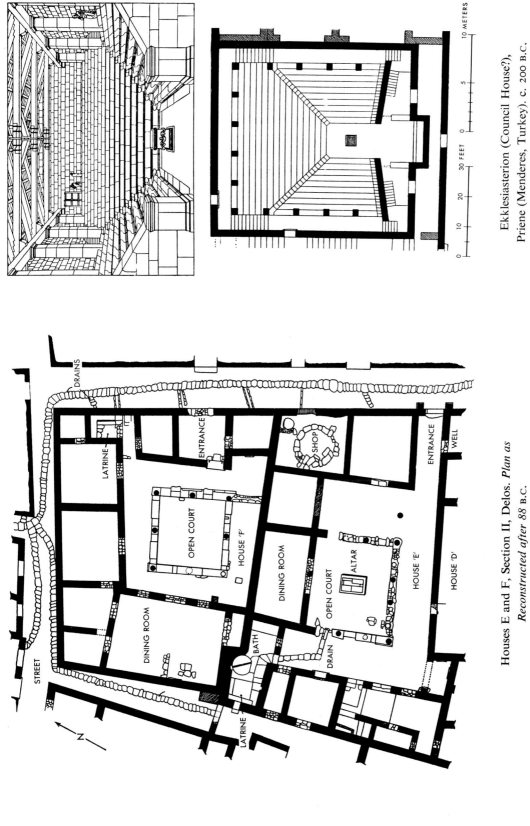

Ekklesiasterion (Council House?),
Priene (Menderes, Turkey). c. 200 B.C.
Restored Interior, and Plan

Houses E and F, Section II, Delos. *Plan as
Reconstructed after 88 B.C.
(same scale as Plan at right)*

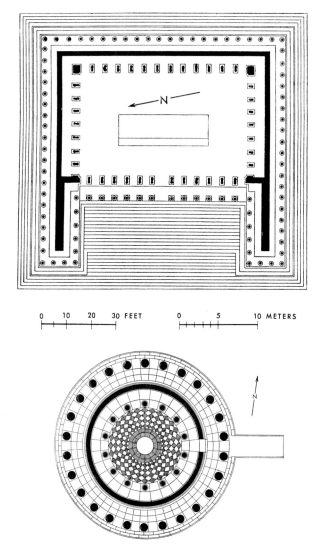

0 10 20 30 FEET   0   5   10 METERS

ABOVE
Altar of Zeus, Pergamum
(Bergama, Turkey).
Begun 180–170 B.C.
*Plan, and Reconstruction
of West Front in
State Museums, Berlin*

LEFT
Tholos, Sanctuary of Asclepius,
Epidaurus. C. 360 B.C. *Plan
(both Plans at same scale)*

105
102
96, 97) 85

GIOVANNI PAOLO PANINI. *The Interior of the Pantheon.* Oil on canvas, 50 1/2 × 39″.
c. 1750 A.D. *National Gallery of Art, Washington, D.C. (Kress Collection)*

Pantheon, Rome. c. 118–25 A.D. *View of Façade from the north*

Theater, Sanctuary of Asclepius, Epidaurus.
c. 350 B.C. *View from northwest, and Plan*

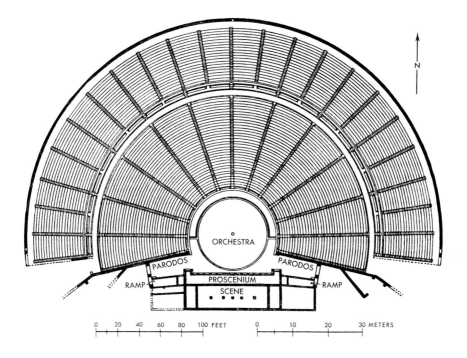

THE ANCIENT WORLD

6. *Etruscan Architecture*

ALL LOCATIONS ARE IN ITALY

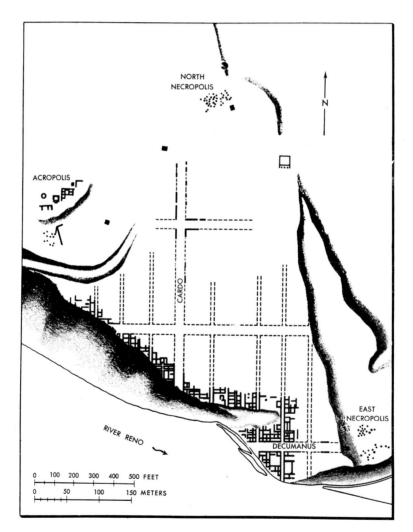

City of Marzabotto, southwest of Bologna.
Late 6th–early 5th centuries B.C. *Plan*

Porta Augusta (City Gate), Perugia. 2nd century B.C. *View of Exterior Façade*

Burial Chamber, "Tomb of the Reliefs," Cerveteri. 4th century B.C.
View showing Stucco Reliefs

THE ANCIENT WORLD

7. *Roman Architecture*

ALL LOCATIONS ARE IN ITALY, UNLESS OTHERWISE SPECIFIED

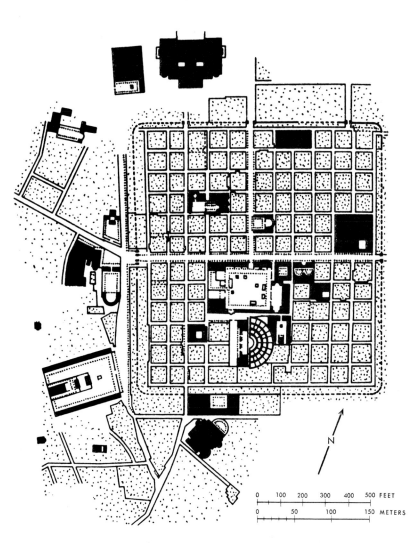

City of Timgad (Algeria). 100–117 A.D. *Plan*

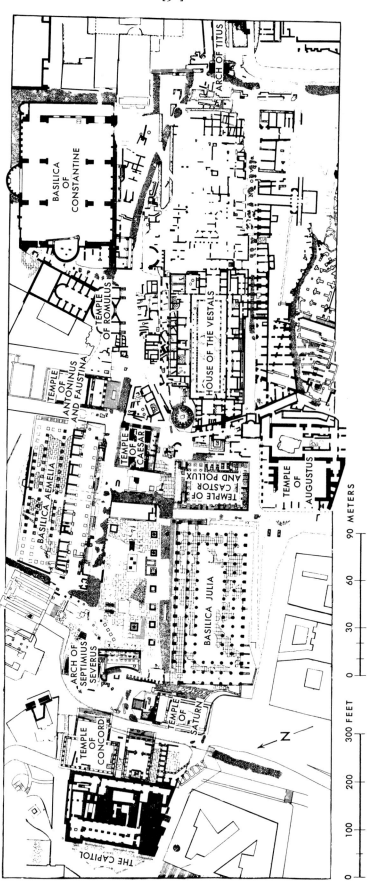

Forum Romanum, Rome. 1st century B.C. to 4th century A.D. *Plan*

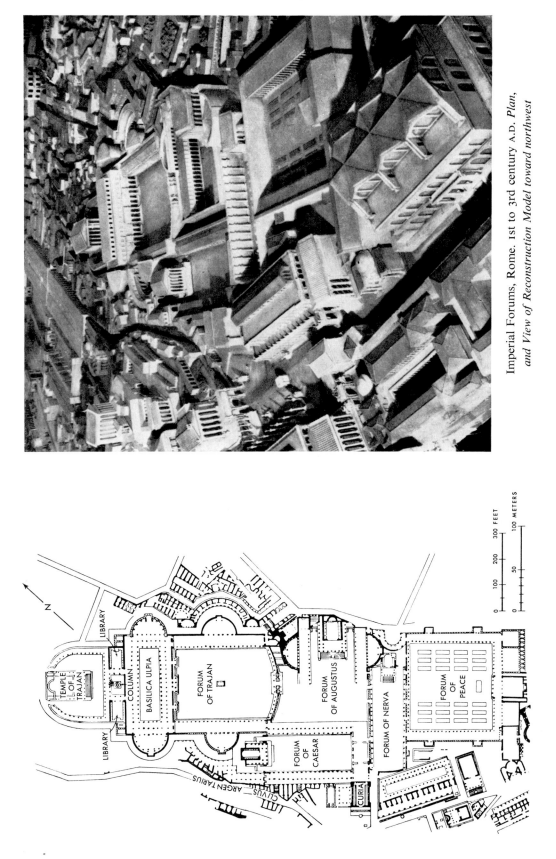

Imperial Forums, Rome. 1st to 3rd century A.D. *Plan, and View of Reconstruction Model toward northwest*

Forum of Trajan, Rome. c. 113–17 A.D.
View of Mercati (Market Buildings) from northeast

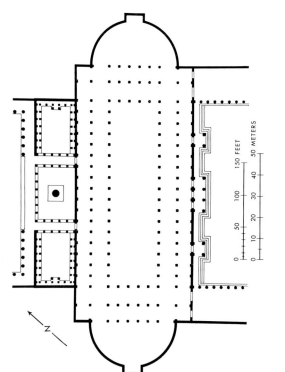

Forum of Trajan, Rome. c. 113–17 A.D.
Plan of Basilica Ulpia

BELOW

Maison Carrée, Nîmes (France). Completed 16 B.C.
View from northeast

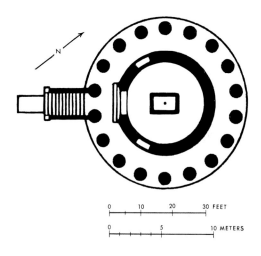

Temple of the Sibyl, Tivoli.
Early 1st century B.C.
View from the north, and Plan

Theater of Marcellus, Rome. 1st century B.C. *View of Exterior from the north, and Plan*

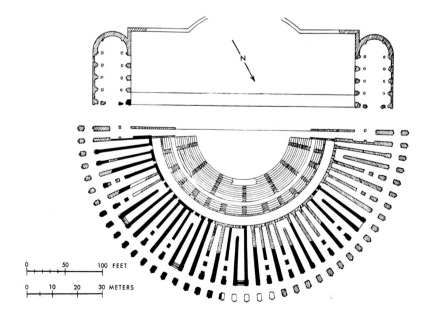

Colosseum, Rome. 72–80 A.D. *Air View from southwest, and Exterior from the north*

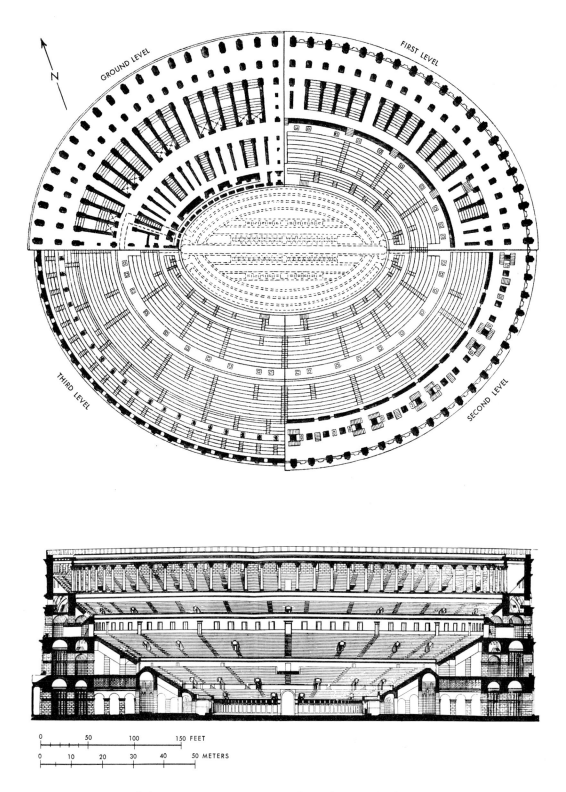

Colosseum, Rome. 72–80 A.D. *Plan and Longitudinal Section*

Temple of Bacchus, Baalbek (Lebanon). 2nd century A.D.
Interior View of Cella Wall

Temple of Venus, Baalbek (Lebanon).
3rd century A.D. *View of Exterior
from the east, and Plan*

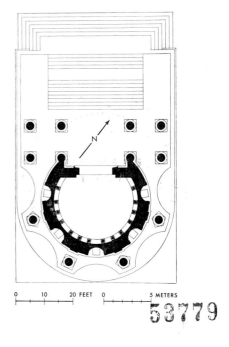

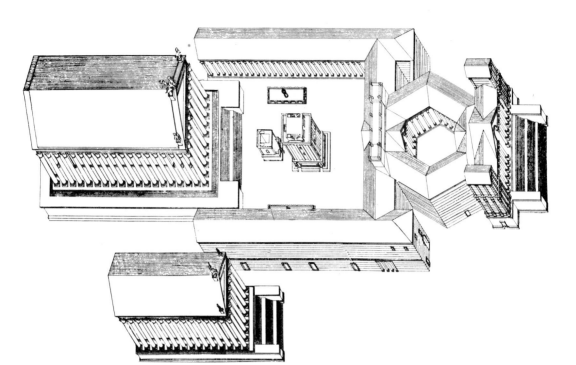

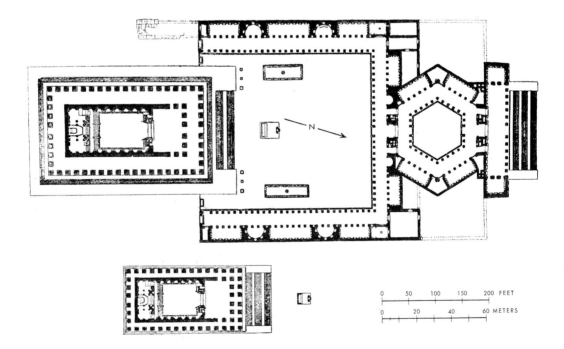

Temple Enclosure, Baalbek (Lebanon). 1st to 2nd century A.D.
Reconstruction Drawing, and Plan

GIOVANNI PAOLO PANINI. *The Interior of the Pantheon.* Oil on canvas, 50 1/2 × 39″.
c. 1750 A.D. *National Gallery of Art, Washington, D.C. (Kress Collection)*

Pantheon, Rome. c. 118–25 A.D. *View of Façade from the north*

Pantheon, Rome.
c. 118–25 A.D.
Structural Diagram

Pantheon, Rome. c. 118–25 A.D. *Plan, and View of Reconstruction Model of Area from northwest*

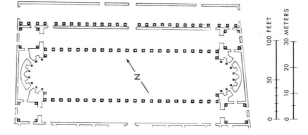

Basilica, Leptis Magna (Libya). Early 3rd century A.D. *Plan, and View of Interior*

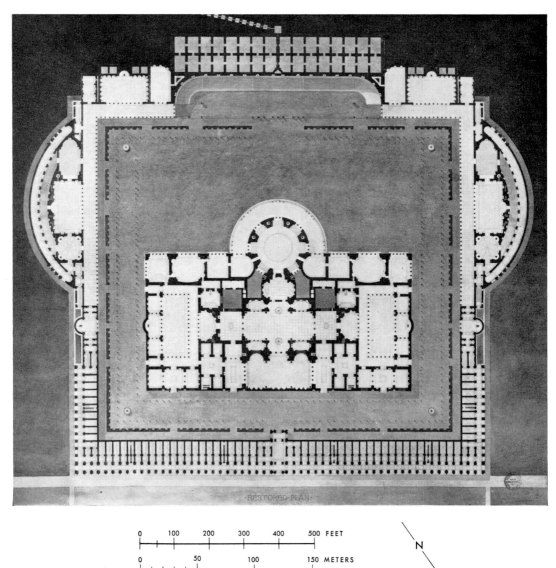

0   100   200   300   400   500 FEET

0   50   100   150 METERS

N

Baths of Caracalla, Rome. 212–23 A.D. *Plan*

Baths of Caracalla, Rome. 212–23 A.D. *Reconstruction Rendering from the north*

Baths of Caracalla, Rome. 212–23 A.D. *Air View from the south*

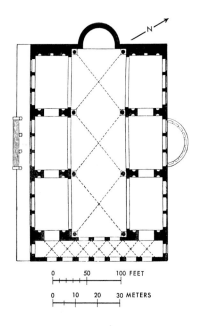

Basilica of Constantine, Rome. c. 310–20 A.D.
View from the south, and Plan

RIGHT
Monumental Arch,
Susa. c. 8 B.C.

BELOW
Arch of Constantine,
Rome. Early 4th
century A.D.

House of the Vettii, Pompeii. c. 50 A.D. *View through Peristyle*

House of Neptune and Amphitrite, Herculaneum. 1st century B.C.
View through Atrium

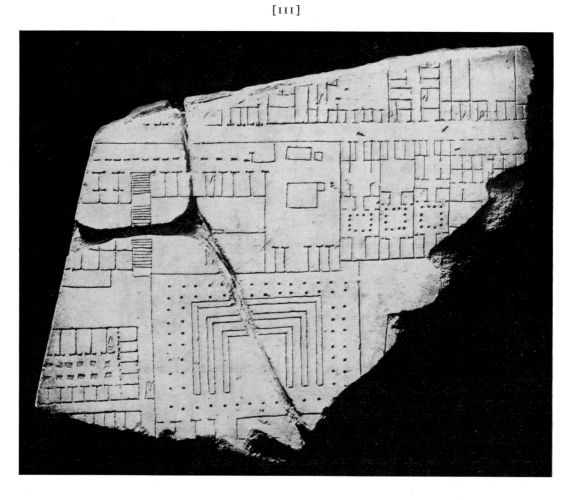

ABOVE
Fragment of *Forma Urbis*
(Plan of Rome). c. 200 A.D.
Museo Comune, Rome

RIGHT
Architectural View, left portion of
wall painting from a villa at
Boscoreale. 1st century B.C.
*The Metropolitan Museum of Art,
New York (Rogers Fund, 1903)*

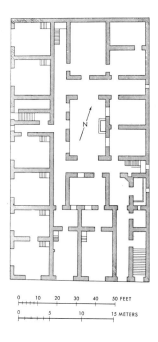

Apartment House (House of Diana), Ostia.
2nd century A.D. *Street Façade and Plan*

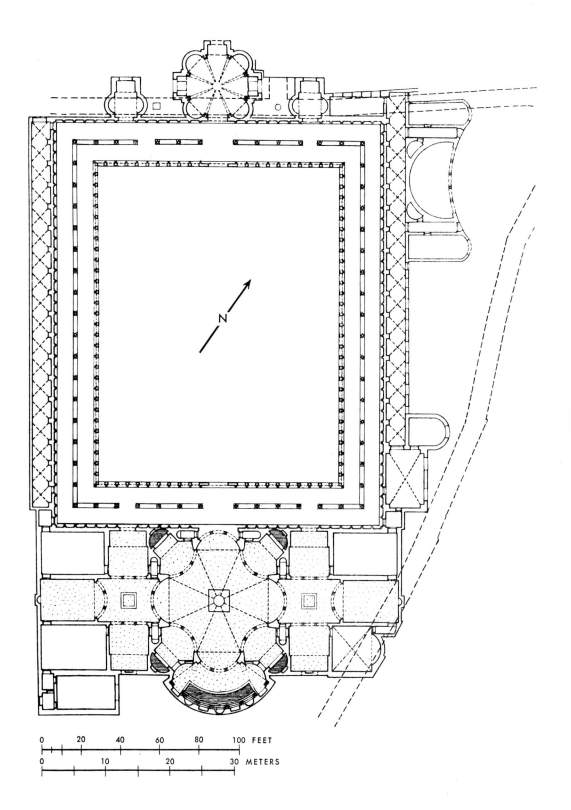

Piazza d'Oro, Hadrian's Villa, Tivoli. 125–35 A.D. *Plan*

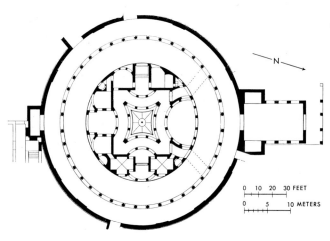

Circular Casino, Hadrian's Villa,
Tivoli. 125–35 A.D. *View and Plan*

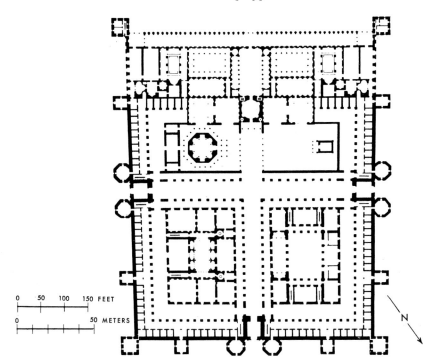

0 50 100 150 FEET

0   50 METERS

N

Palace of Diocletian, Split (Yugoslavia). c. 300 A.D. *Plan (engraved 1764 A.D.*
by Robert Adam), and View of Ceremonial Court from the north

Mausoleum, Palace of Diocletian, Split (Yugoslavia). c. 300 A.D.
Interior View (engraved 1764 A.D. by Robert Adam)

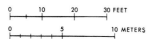

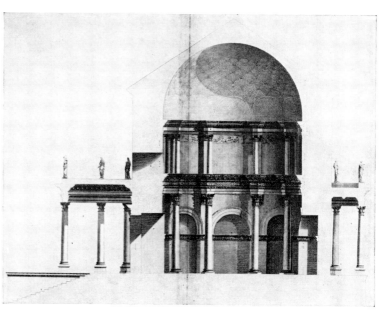

Palace of Diocletian,
Split (Yugoslavia).
c. 300 A.D. *Longitudinal
Section of Mausoleum,
and View of East
Gate of Palace*

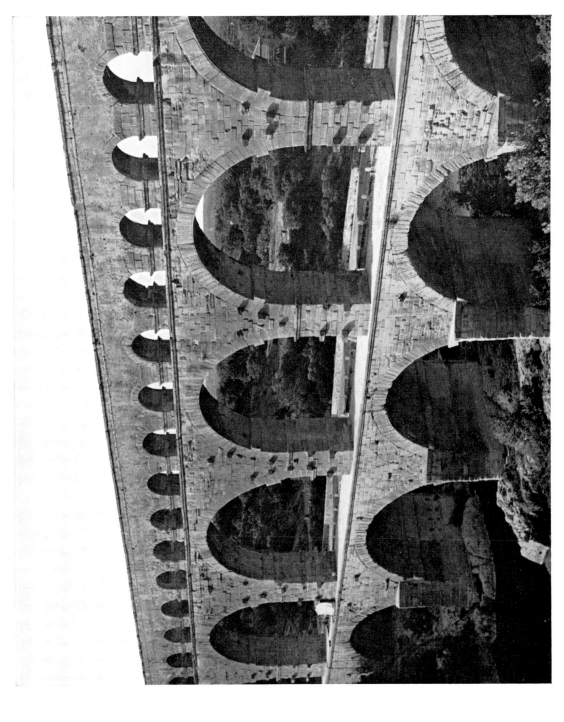

Pont du Gard
(viaduct and aqueduct),
near Nîmes (France).
Early 1st century A.D.
View from northwest

BELOW
Market Gate, Miletus
(Palatia, Turkey).
c. 160 A.D.
Reconstruction in
State Museums, Berlin

Porta Nigra (fortified city gate), Trier (Germany).
Early 4th century A.D. *View of Exterior Façade*

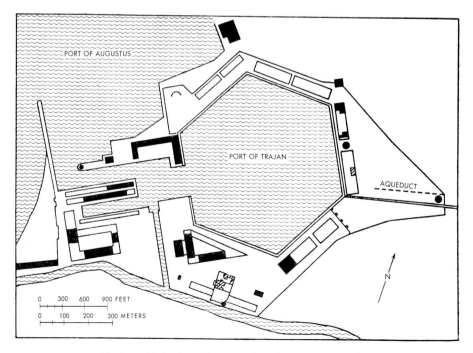

Harbor, Ostia. Largely 1st and 2nd century A.D. *Plan*

THE ANCIENT WORLD

8. *Early Christian Architecture*

ALL DATES ARE A.D.

S. Costanza, Rome. c. 350. *View of Interior toward southwest*

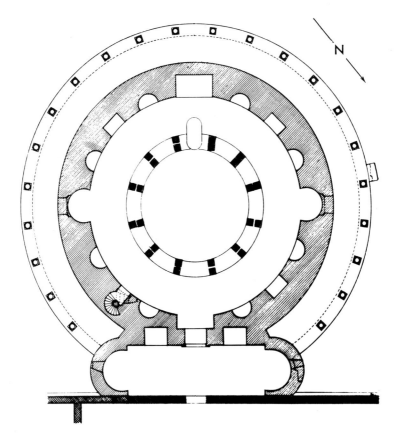

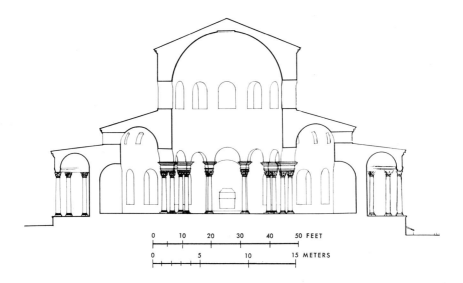

S. Costanza, Rome. c. 350. *Plan and Transverse Section*

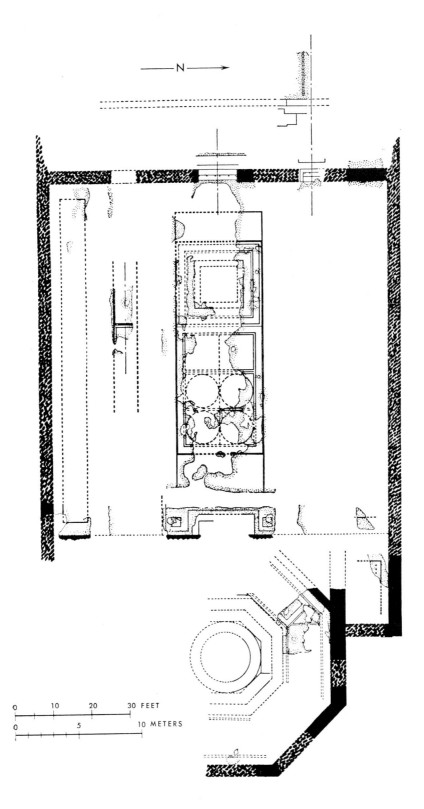

Church of the Nativity, Bethlehem (Bayt Laḥm, Jordan). Begun c. 326.
Plan of Original Building

S. Stefano Rotondo, Rome. 468–83.
View of Interior, and Plan

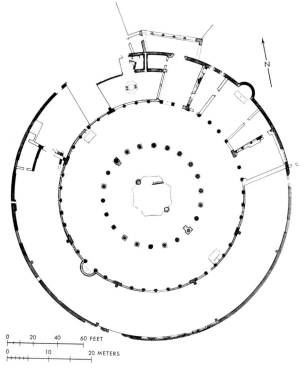

Church, Qalb Lauzeh (Syria). c. 500.
View of Exterior Wall and Apse, and Plan

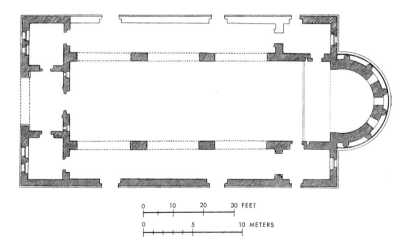

Basilica, Trier (Germany). Early 4th century. *View of Exterior*

Old St. Peter's,
Vatican City (Rome).
c. 333. *Interior toward Apse,*
as shown in 16th-century
fresco on nave wall of
S. Martino ai Monti, Rome

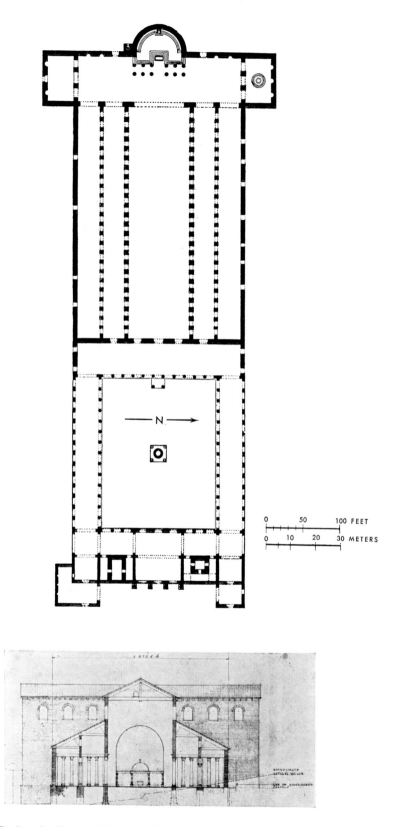

Old St. Peter's, Vatican City (Rome). c. 333. *Plan and Transverse Section*

S. Maria Maggiore, Rome. 432–40. *View of Interior toward northwest (ceiling c. 1500)*

Mausoleum of Galla Placidia, Ravenna (Italy). c. 450. *Exterior from the west*

ABOVE
S. Apollinare Nuovo,
Ravenna (Italy). c. 520.
*Interior View of
South Wall of Nave*

LEFT
S. Apollinare in Classe
(near Ravenna, Italy).
c. 530–49. *Air View
from southwest*

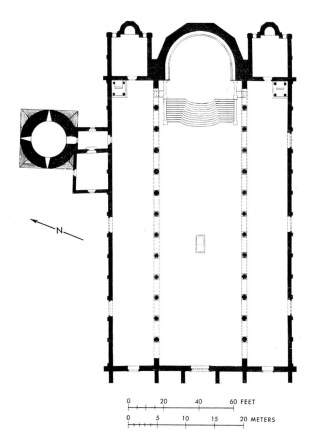

S. Apollinare in Classe
(near Ravenna, Italy).
c. 530–49. *View of
Interior toward
the east, and Plan*

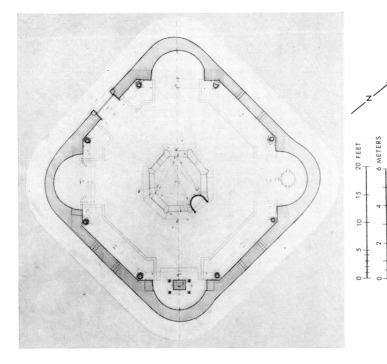

Baptistery of the Orthodox, Ravenna (Italy).
First half of 5th century. *View of Interior, and Plan*

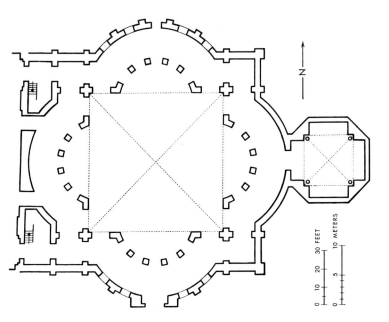

ABOVE
S. Lorenzo Maggiore, Milan (Italy). c. 480. *Plan*

RIGHT
Baptistery of the Orthodox, Ravenna (Italy).
First half of 5th century. *Exterior from southwest*

THE ANCIENT WORLD

9. *Byzantine Architecture*

ALL DATES ARE A.D.

S. Vitale, Ravenna (Italy). 526–47. *View of Interior including Apse, from the east*

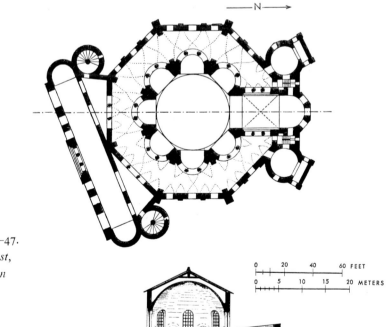

S. Vitale, Ravenna (Italy). 526–47.
View of Exterior from northeast,
Plan, and Longitudinal Section

SS. Sergius and Bacchus, Istanbul (Turkey). c. 527. *View of Interior*

SS. Sergius and Bacchus, Istanbul (Turkey). c. 527.
Plan and Longitudinal Section

ANTHEMIUS OF TRALLES and ISIDORUS OF MILETUS. Hagia Sophia, Istanbul (Turkey).
532–37. *View of Exterior from southwest*

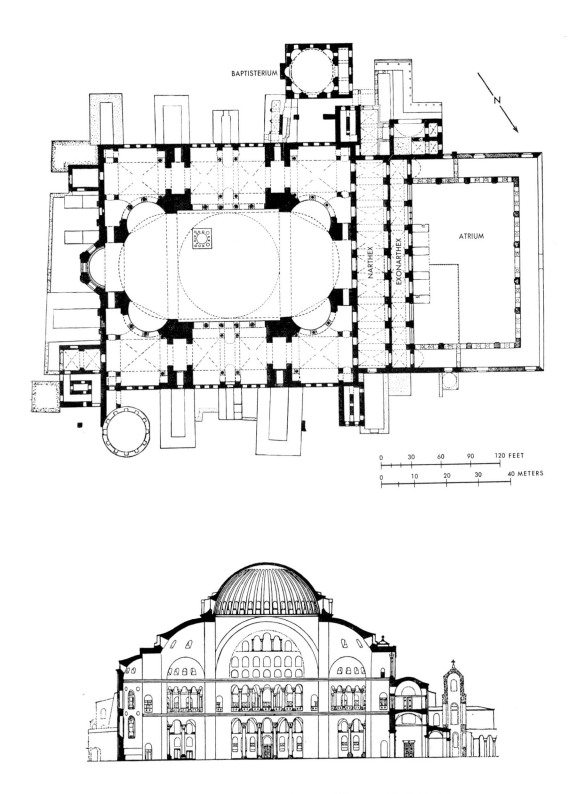

ANTHEMIUS OF TRALLES and ISIDORUS OF MILETUS. Hagia Sophia,
Istanbul (Turkey). 532–37. *Plan, and Longitudinal Section*

ANTHEMIUS OF TRALLES and ISIDORUS OF MILETUS. Hagia Sophia,
Istanbul (Turkey). 532–37. *View of Interior toward Apse (southeast)*

ANTHEMIUS OF TRALLES and ISIDORUS OF MILETUS. Hagia Sophia,
Istanbul (Turkey). 532–37. *View of Interior toward the east*

Churches of St. Luke of Stiris (left) and of the Virgin (right), Monastery of Hosios Loukas, Phocis (Greece). Early 11th century. *Exterior View from the east*

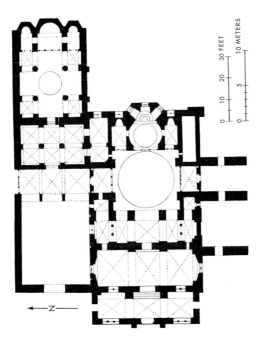

Church of St. Luke of Stiris,
Monastery of Hosios Loukas,
Phocis (Greece). Early 11th century.
View of Interior toward the east, and Plan

Church of the Dormition, Vladimir (Russia). 1158–61; rebuilt 1185–89. *Exterior View of Apse*

Cathedral of St. Basil, Moscow (Russia). 1554–60. *Exterior View from southwest*

PART TWO

ASIA AND AMERICA

10. *Islamic Architecture*

11. *Architecture of Indian Asia*

12. *Chinese and Japanese Architecture*

13. *American Architecture before Columbus*

LIST OF ILLUSTRATIONS

10. ISLAMIC ARCHITECTURE

page 149 Great Mosque of Mutawakkil, Samarra (Iraq). 847–52. *Air View* (courtesy Clarendon Press, Oxford)

150 Palace, Mshatta (Jordan). 743–50; unfinished. *Portion of South Façade* (State Museums, Berlin)

151 Great Mosque, Cordova (Spain). 786–87. *Interior of Sanctuary* (Kidder Smith)

151 Great Mosque, Cordova (Spain). *Plan, including later additions*

152 Chapel of Villaviciosa, Great Mosque, Cordova (Spain). 961–65. *View into Lantern* (Kidder Smith)

153 Court of the Lions, Palace of the Alhambra, Granada (Spain). 1354–91. *View toward the east* (Kidder Smith)

154 Hall of the Two Sisters, Palace of the Alhambra, Granada (Spain). 1354–91. *View into Dome* (Mas)

155 Madrasa of Sultan Hasan, Cairo (Egypt). 1356–63. *South Façade of Adjoining Tomb Chamber* (Kidder Smith)

155 Madrasa of Sultan Hasan, Cairo (Egypt). 1356–63. *Interior Court of Mosque* (Kidder Smith)

156 Maidan-i-Shah (Royal Square), Isfahan (Iran). Late 16th century. *Air View* (Dr. Erich Schmidt)

156 Masjid-i-Jami, Isfahan (Iran). 15th century. *Plan* (Pope, II, fig. 328)

157 Masjid-i-Jami, Isfahan (Iran). 15th century. *Rear View of Northwest Ivan* (courtesy Arthur Upham Pope)

158 The Ark, Masjid-i-Ali Shah, Tabriz (Iran). Early 14th century. *View from the west* (composite photograph, courtesy Arthur Upham Pope)

159 Mosque of Ahmed I, Istanbul (Turkey). 1609–16. *South Façade* (Kidder Smith)

160 Taj Mahal (mausoleum), Agra (India). 1630–48. *View from the south* (Tiers, Monkmeyer Press Photo Svce., N. Y.)

161 Masjid-i-Shah, Isfahan (Iran). 1616. *Outer Portal* (Pope, II, fig. 517)

161 Farahabad Gardens, Summer Residence of Shah Sultan Husayn, Isfahan (Iran). c. 1700. *Plan*

11. ARCHITECTURE OF INDIAN ASIA

162 Stūpa No. 1, Sānchī (India). 3rd to early 1st century B.C. *View from the east* (Gov't of India, Dept. of Archaeology)

163 Stūpa No. 1, Sānchī (India). Early 1st century B.C. *North Gate* (Elisofon)

164 Cave No. 19, Ajanta (India). Early 6th century A.D. *Façade of Chaitya-Hall* (Elisofon)

164 Temple No. 17, Sānchī (India). Early 5th century A.D. *Façade* (Gov't of India, Dept. of Archaeology)

165 Great Temple Compound, Bhuvaneshwar (India). c. 1000 A.D. *General View* (Elisofon)

166 Sanctuary, Borobudur (Central Java, Indonesia). Late 8th to 9th century A.D. *Air View* (courtesy Fogg Art Museum)

166 Shrine of Angkor Wat (Cambodia). Early 12th century A.D. *Air View* (Elisofon)

12. CHINESE AND JAPANESE ARCHITECTURE

page 167 Sanctuary, Inner Shrine, Ise (Japan). Traditional since 3rd century; this example c. 1900. *Exterior* (Benrido Co., Kyoto)

168 Model of House. Chinese, 1st century (Han Dynasty). *Nelson-Atkins Gallery, Kansas City, Mo.* (Museum)

169 Pagoda, Daigoji, Kyoto (Japan). 951. *Exterior View* (Asukaen, Nara)

170 Monastery, Horyuji (Japan). 7th century. *Courtyard and Middle Gate* (Asukaen, Nara)

171 Kondo (Main Hall), Toshodaiji, Nara (Japan). Late 8th century. *Interior, and Detail of Bracketing* (Asukaen, Nara; A. C. Soper, *The Evolution... Japan*, Princeton, 1942)

172 Hoodo (Phoenix Hall), Byodoin Temple, Uji (near Kyoto, Japan). 11th century. *Exterior View* (Asukaen, Nara)

173 *Construction Methods*, from Japanese scroll *Matsuzaki-tenjin-engi*. 1311. *National Museum, Tokyo* (Museum)

174 *House of a Priest*, from Japanese scroll *Kasuga-gongen-reikenke*. 1309. *National Museum, Tokyo* (courtesy Prof. A. C. Soper, Institute of Fine Arts, N.Y.)

174 *House of a Lesser Nobleman*, from Japanese scroll *Ishiyamadera-engi*. 14th century. *National Museum, Tokyo* (courtesy Prof. A. C. Soper, Institute of Fine Arts, N.Y.)

175 LI JUNG-CHIN. *A Pleasure Palace*, Chinese hanging scroll. Yüan Dynasty (1260–1368). *National Palace Museum, Peking* (courtesy Prof. A. C. Soper, Institute of Fine Arts, N.Y.)

176 Himeji Castle, Hyogo (Japan.) 1573–1615. *Exterior* (courtesy City Hall, Himeji)

177 Imperial Palace, Peking (China). 15th century, with additions through 17th century. *Exterior of Grand Ancestral Shrine, and Plan* (courtesy Prof. A. C. Soper, Institute of Fine Arts, N.Y.; Lurçat, fig. 25)

178 Shokintei Tea Pavilion, Katsura Imperial Palace, Kyoto (Japan). 17th century. *Exterior* (T. Sato, courtesy Prof. A. C. Soper, Institute of Fine Arts, N.Y.)

178 Kuro-shoin (hall with desk alcove), Nishi Honganji, Kyoto (Japan). Late 16th century. *Interior of Alcove* (Benrido Co., Kyoto)

13. AMERICAN ARCHITECTURE BEFORE COLUMBUS

179 Pyramid of the Sun, Teotihuacan (Mexico). Aztec, c. 100. *General View* (courtesy Amer. Mus. of Nat. Hist., N. Y.)

180 Teotihuacan (Mexico). Aztec and Maya, 1st millennium. *Plan, and Detailed Plan* (R. Millon & J. H. Bennyhoff, *American Antiquity*, XXVI, 4, 1961, fig. 1)

181 Temple of Quetzalcoatl, Citadel, Teotihuacan (Mexico). Maya, 9th century. *View* (Instituto Nacional de Antropologia e Storia, Mexico City)

182 Palace and Temple, Labna (Yucatan, Mexico). Maya, 11th–12th century. *General View* (courtesy Loring Hewen, N. Y.)

183 Pyramid and Temple of the Warriors, Chichén Itzá (Yucatan, Mexico). Toltec, 11th century. *General View, and West Façade of Temple* (Laura Gilpin, Santa Fé; Carnegie Institution of Washington, D. C.)

184 Nunnery Quadrangle, Uxmal (Yucatan, Mexico). Maya, 9th–10th century. *Exterior* (Amer. Mus. of Nat. Hist., N. Y.)

184 Chichén Itzá (Yucatan, Mexico). Toltec, 11th century. *Plan of Central Section* (Kubler, *Art and Architecture in Ancient America*, fig. 55)

185 Chan-Chan, Moche Valley (Peru). Chimú, founded c. 1000. *Air View and General Plan* (courtesy Wenner-Gren Foundation; Kubler, *Art and Architecture in Ancient America*, fig. 97)

186 Citadel, Machu Picchu (Peru). Inca, 15th century. *Domestic Buildings* (Holton, Photo Library, Inc.)

187 Citadel, Machu Picchu (Peru). Inca, 15th century. *Upper Buildings* (George Pinney, Photo Library, Inc.)

188 Ollantaytambo (Peru). Inca, 15th century. *Masonry Wall* (Prof. H. Ubbelohde-Doering, Lima)

188 "Gate of the Sun," Tiahuanaco (Bolivia). Pre-Inca, c. 1000–1300. *View* (Grace Line)

ASIA AND AMERICA

10. *Islamic Architecture*

ALL DATES ARE A.D.

Great Mosque of Mutawakkil, Samarra (Iraq). 847–52. *Air View*

Palace, Mshatta (Jordan). 743–50; unfinished. Height of triangles 9 1/2′.
Portion of South Façade

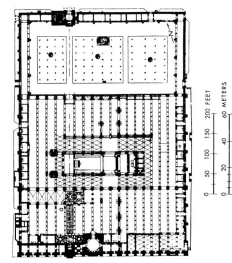

Great Mosque, Cordova (Spain). 786–87.
Plan (including later additions),
and Interior View of Sanctuary from the east

Chapel of Villaviciosa, Great Mosque, Cordova (Spain). 961–65.
*View from the east into Lantern (*a *on Plan, preceding page)*

Court of the Lions, Palace of the Alhambra, Granada (Spain). 1354–91.
View toward the east (fountain 11th century)

Hall of the Two Sisters, Palace of the Alhambra, Granada (Spain). 1354–91.
View into Dome, showing Stucco Decorations

Madrasa of Sultan Hasan, Cairo (Egypt). 1356–63.
View of Interior Court of Mosque, from Qibla Side

Madrasa of Sultan Hasan, Cairo (Egypt). 1356–63.
South Façade Adjoining of Tomb Chamber

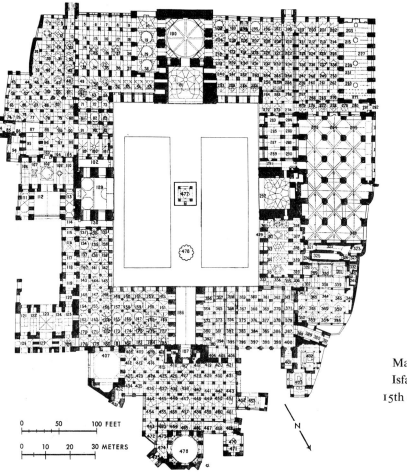

Maidan-i-Shah (Royal Square), Isfahan (Iran). Late 16th century. *Air View from southeast*

Masjid-i-Jami,
Isfahan (Iran).
15th century. *Plan*

0   50   100 FEET

0   10   20   30 METERS

N

Masjid-i-Jami, Isfahan (Iran). 15th century. *Rear View of Northwest Ivan*
(porch recessed from central court)

The Ark, Masjid-i-Ali Shah, Tabriz (Iran). Early 14th century.
View from the west (composite photograph)

Mosque of Ahmed I, Istanbul (Turkey). 1609–16. *View of South Façade*

Taj Mahal (mausoleum), Agra (India). 1630–48. *View from the south*

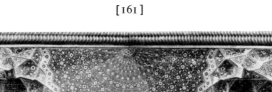

ABOVE
Masjid-i-Shah,
Isfahan (Iran). 1616.
View into Outer Portal

RIGHT
Farahabad Gardens,
Summer Residence of
Shah Sultan Husayn,
Isfahan (Iran).
c. 1700. *Plan*

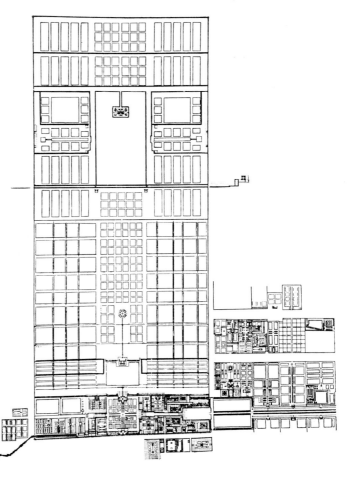

ASIA AND AMERICA

11. Architecture of
Indian Asia

Stūpa No. 1, Sānchī (India). 3rd to early 1st century B.C.
View from the east

Stūpa No. 1, Sānchī (India). Early 1st century B.C.
Exterior of North Gate

Cave No. 19, Ajanta (India). Early 6th century A.D.
Façade of Rock-Cut Chaitya-Hall

Temple No. 17, Sānchī (India).
Early 5th century A.D.
View of Façade

Great Temple Compound, Bhuvaneshwar (India). c. 1000 A.D. *General View*

Sanctuary, Borobudur (Central Java, Indonesia). Late 8th to 9th century A.D.
Air View from the north

Shrine of Angkor Wat (Cambodia). Early 12th century A.D.
Air View from the north

ASIA AND AMERICA

12. Chinese and

Japanese Architecture

ALL DATES ARE A.D.

Sanctuary, Inner Shrine, Ise (Japan). Traditional since 3rd century;
this example c. 1900. *Exterior from the south*

Model of House. Chinese, 1st century (Han Dynasty). Painted pottery,
height 52″. *Nelson-Atkins Gallery, Kansas City, Mo.*

Pagoda (five-storied tower), Daigoji, Kyoto (Japan). 951. *Exterior View*

Monastery, Horyuji (Japan). 7th century. *General View of*
Courtyard from above (southeast), and Middle Gate

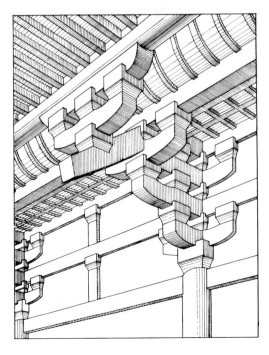

Kondo (Main Hall), Toshodaiji,
Nara (Japan). Late 8th century.
View of Interior, and Detail of Bracketing

Hoodo (Phoenix Hall), Byodoin Temple, Uji (near Kyoto, Japan).
11th century. *Exterior View*

Construction Methods, from Japanese scroll *Matsuzaki-tenjin-engi*.
Ink and color on silk, 1311. *National Museum, Tokyo*

House of a Priest, from Japanese scroll *Kasuga-gongen-reikenke*. Ink and color on silk, 1309. *National Museum, Tokyo*

House of a Lesser Nobleman, from Japanese scroll *Ishiyamadera-engi*. Ink and color on silk, 14th century. *National Museum, Tokyo*

LI JUNG-CHIN. *A Pleasure Palace*, Chinese hanging scroll. Ink and color on silk,
Yüan Dynasty (1260–1368). *National Palace Museum, Peking*

Himeji Castle, Hyogo (Japan). 1573–1615. *Exterior View including Fortifications*

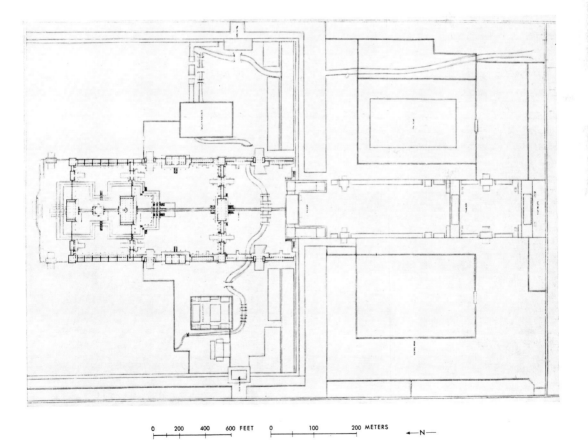

0 200 400 600 FEET   0   100   200 METERS   ← N —

Imperial Palace, Peking (China). 15th century, with additions through
17th century. *Exterior of Grand Ancestral Shrine (T'ai-miao), and General Plan*

Shokintei ("Arbor of Soughing Pines") Tea Pavilion, Katsura Imperial Palace,
Kyoto (Japan). 17th century. *General Exterior View*

Kuro-shoin (hall with desk alcove), Nishi Honganji, Kyoto (Japan).
Late 16th century. *Interior of Alcove*

ASIA AND AMERICA

13. American Architecture before Columbus

ALL DATES ARE A.D.

Pyramid of the Sun, Teotihuacan (Mexico). Aztec, c. 100.
Height 216'. *General View*

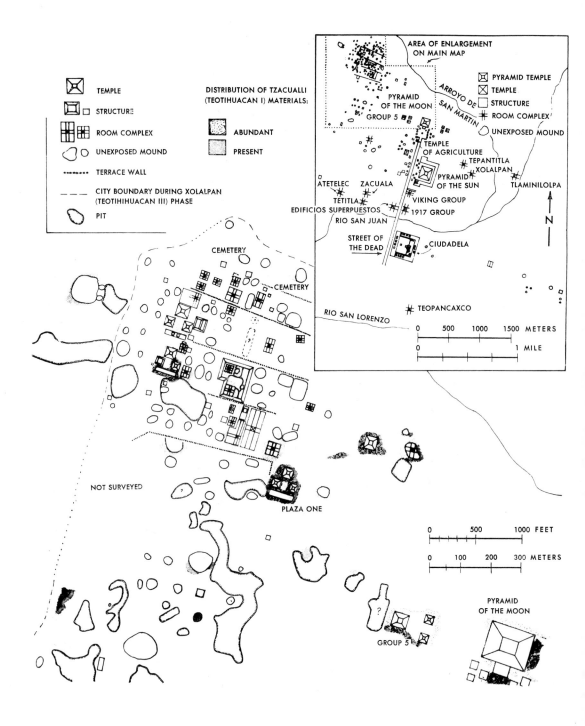

Teotihuacan (Mexico). Aztec and Maya, 1st millennium
General Plan, and Detailed Plan of Southwest Area

Temple of Quetzalcoatl, Citadel, Teotihuacan (Mexico).
Maya, 9th century. *View from the south*

Palace and Temple, Labna (Yucatan, Mexico). Maya, 11th–12th century. *General View*

Pyramid and Temple of the Warriors, Chichén Itzá (Yucatan, Mexico). Toltec, 11th century.
General View from the west (below), and West Façade of Temple (above)

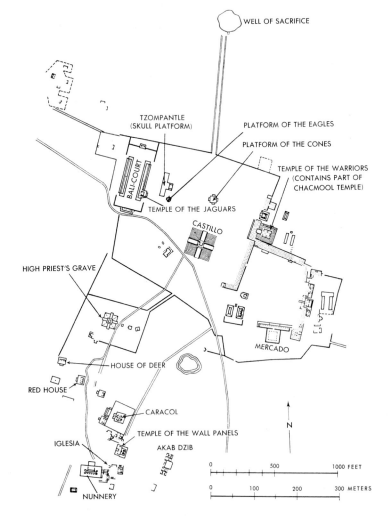

ABOVE
Nunnery Quadrangle,
Uxmal (Yucatan, Mexico).
Maya, 9th–10th century.
Exterior View

RIGHT
Chichén Itzá
(Yucatan, Mexico).
Toltec, 11th century.
Plan of Central Section

WELL OF SACRIFICE

TZOMPANTLE
(SKULL PLATFORM)

PLATFORM OF THE EAGLES

PLATFORM OF THE CONES

TEMPLE OF THE WARRIORS
(CONTAINS PART OF
CHACMOOL TEMPLE)

BALL-COURT

TEMPLE OF THE JAGUARS

CASTILLO

HIGH PRIEST'S GRAVE

MERCADO

HOUSE OF DEER

RED HOUSE

CARACOL

TEMPLE OF THE WALL PANELS

IGLESIA

AKAB DZIB

N

NUNNERY

0   500   1000 FEET

0   100   200   300 METERS

Chan-Chan, Moche Valley
(Peru). Chimú,
founded c. 1000.
*Air View of Compounds,
and General Plan*

0 1000 3000 5000 FEET

0 500 1000 1500 METERS

N

UHLE GROUP

RIVERO GROUP
(SECOND PALACE)

TSCHUDI GROUP
(FIRST PALACE)

Citadel, Machu Picchu (Peru).
Inca, 15th century.
View of Domestic Buildings

BELOW
Citadel, Machu Picchu (Peru).
Inca, 15th century.
View of Upper Buildings

ABOVE
Ollantaytambo (Peru).
Inca, 15th century.
Portion of Masonry Wall

LEFT
"Gate of the Sun",
Tiahuanaco (Bolivia).
Pre-Inca, c. 1000–1300.
View from the north

PART THREE

THE MIDDLE AGES

LIST OF ILLUSTRATIONS

14. EARLY MEDIEVAL ARCHITECTURE

page 195 Gatehouse, Monastery, Lorsch (Germany). 767–74. *Façade* (Schmidt-Glassner)

196 St. Riquier, Centula (Picardy, France). Consecrated 799. *Engraving by Petau, 1612* (Bibliothèque Nationale, Paris)

196 Palace of Charlemagne, Ingelheim (Germany). 774–87. *Plan* (C. Rauch, *Die Pfalz... am Rhein*, Münster, 1930, fig. 1)

197 Palatine Chapel, Aachen (Germany). 792–805. *Façade* (Marburg)

198 Palatine Chapel, Aachen (Germany). 792–805. *Interior* (SBB)

199 Palace of Charlemagne and Palatine Chapel, Aachen (Germany). c. 790–805. *General Plan, and Longitudinal Section* (Conant, fig. 1)

200 *Plan for a Monastery.* c. 820. Chapter Library, St. Gall (Switzerland) (Zumbühl)

201 S. Maria, Ripoll (Catalonia, Spain). *Exterior (after reconstruction), and Plan* (Mas; J. Puig i Cadafalch, *Géographie... Art Roman)*

202 St. Michael, Hildesheim (Germany). 1001–1033. *Interior* (SBB)

203 St. Michael, Hildesheim (Germany). 1001–1033. *Plan and Longitudinal Section (both reconstructed after* Beseler)

204 Ste. Gertrude, Nivelles (Belgium). 1000–1046. *Interior and Plan* (ACL; A. Mottart, *La Collégiale... Nivelles)*

205 West Tower, Earl's Barton (Northamptonshire, England). c. 1000. *Exterior* (Kersting)

15. ROMANESQUE ARCHITECTURE

206 Cathedral, Pisa (Italy). Begun 1063. *Interior* (Alinari)

207 Cathedral Square, Pisa (Italy). *General Plan, View, and Plan of Cathedral* (W. Braunfels, *Mittelalterliche... Toscana*, pl. III; Kidder Smith)

208 Basilica of St. Mark, Venice (Italy). 1063–94. *West Façade* (Kidder Smith)

209 Basilica of St. Mark, Venice (Italy). 1063–94. *Air View* (Fotocielo)

210 Basilica of St. Mark, Venice (Italy). 1063–94. *Interior and Plan* (Anderson; Opera di San Marco, Venice)

211 S. Ambrogio, Milan (Italy). Late 11th–12th century. *Interior and Exterior* (Alinari)

212 S. Ambrogio, Milan (Italy). Late 11th–12th century. *Plan and Longitudinal Section* (F. de Dartein, *Étude... lombarde*, pls. 27, 29)

213 Third Abbey Church and Monastery, Cluny (France). 1088–c. 1121. *View* (Bibliothèque Nationale, Paris)

213 Third Abbey Church and Monastery, Cluny (France). 1088–c 1121. *Plan.* (Conant, fig. 31)

214 St. Étienne (Abbaye-aux-Hommes), Caen (France). c. 1068. *West Façade* (Roubier)

215 St. Étienne (Abbaye-aux-Hommes), Caen (France). c. 1068; vaulted c. 1115–20. *Interior and Plan* (Roubier; Conant, fig. 75)

216 St. Philibert, Tournus (France). c. 960–1120. *Nave Arcade* (Arch. Phot.)

217 St. Philibert, Tournus (France). *Exterior* (Arch. Phot.)

218 St. Savin sur Gartempe (France). c. 1095–1115. *Interior* (Roubier)

219 Cathedral of St. Lazare, Autun (France). c. 1120–32. *North Wall of Nave* (Roubier)

220 Notre Dame la Grande, Poitiers (France). c. 1130–45. *West Façade* (courtesy Thames & Hudson, Ltd., London)

221 Cathedral of St. Front, Périgueux (France). c. 1125–50. *Air View* (CAF)

page 222 Cathedral of St. Front, Périgueux (France). c. 1125–50. *Interior and Plan* (Roubier; Conant, fig. 42)

223 St. Sernin, Toulouse (France). c. 1080–1120. *Interior* (Roubier)

224 St. Sernin, Toulouse (France). c. 1080–1120. *Air View and Plan* (YAN; Conant, fig. 28, no. 4)

225 Cathedral, Winchester (England). c. 1090. *Interior* (Felton)

226 Cathedral, Durham (England). 1093–1133. *Interior* (Kersting)

227 Cathedral, Durham (England). 1093–1133. *Plan and Transverse Section* (Conant, figs. 78, 79)

228 St. Mary in Capitol, Cologne (Germany). c. 1030–after 1069. *Exterior* (Marburg)

229 St. Mary in Capitol, Cologne (Germany). c. 1030–after 1069. *Interior and Plan* (Schmölz and Ulrich, Cologne; Conant, fig. 67)

230 Cathedral, Speyer (Germany). Begun 1030. *Plan and Interior, from early 19th-century engraving, before restoration* (Conant, fig. 22; courtesy Institute of Fine Arts, N.Y.)

231 Cathedral, Tournai (France). *Exterior* (ACL)

16. GOTHIC ARCHITECTURE

232 Abbey Church, St. Denis (France). 1140–44. *Ambulatory* (Pierre Devinoy, Paris)

233 Abbey Church, St. Denis (France). 1140–44. *West Façade and Plan* (courtesy Prof. Sumner McK. Crosby, Yale University)

234 Cathedral of Notre Dame, Paris (France). 1163–c. 1250. *West Façade and Plan* (Ward; T. King, *Studybook... Architecture)*

235 Cathedral of Notre Dame, Paris (France). 1163–c. 1250. *Interior* (Roubier)

236 Cathedral of Notre Dame, Paris (France). 1163–c. 1250. *Exterior* (Kidder Smith)

237 Cathedral, Chartres (France). 1194–1220. *Interior, Transverse Section, and Plan* (Marburg; M. Aubert, *La Cathédrale de Chartres;* T. King, *Studybook... Architecture)*

238 Cathedral, Amiens (France). *Choir Vaults* (Kidder Smith)

239 Cathedral, Amiens (France). *Exterior* (Kidder Smith)

240 Cathedral, Amiens (France). *Rose Window* (Foucault)

240 Cathedral, Amiens (France). 1220–88. *Plan and Transverse Section* (Pollitzer)

241 Cathedral, Beauvais (France). Begun 1247. *Air View* (IGN)

241 Cathedral, Beauvais (France). *Reconstruction of First Design, c. 1225* (courtesy Prof. Robert Branner, Columbia University)

242 Cathedral, Beauvais (France). Begun 1247. *Interior* (Ward)

243 Cathedral, Reims (France). c. 1225–99. *West Façade* (Marburg)

244 VILLARD DE HONNECOURT. Three Apse Designs (Bibliothèque Nationale, Paris)

245 JAN VAN EYCK. *St. Barbara before a Gothic Tower.* 1437. *Royal Museum of Fine Arts, Antwerp* (ACL)

246 Pont St. Bénézet, Avignon (France). 1177–85. *View* (Arch. Phot.)

246 Ramparts, Aigues-Mortes (France). 1240–72. *Outer View* (Jeiter)

247 Cathedral, Salisbury (England). 1220–70. *Exterior* (Edwin Smith)

248 Cathedral, Salisbury (England). 1220–70. *Interior and Plan* (F. H. Crossley, NBR; Grigson, *English Cathedrals*, p. 31)

249 Church of Our Lady (Liebfrauenkirche), Trier (Germany). 1235–c. 1253. *West Façade* (SBB)

250 Church of Our Lady (Liebfrauenkirche), Trier (Germany). 1235–c. 1253. *Interior and Plan* (SBB)

251 Abbey, Fossanova (Priverno, Italy). Consecrated 1208. *Exterior* (Fototeca Unione)

252 Abbey, Fossanova (Priverno, Italy). Consecrated 1208. *Interior and Plan* (courtesy Prof. H. W. Janson, New York University)

253 Cathedral, Siena (Italy). Completed c. 1264. *Interior* (Anderson)

254 S. Croce, Florence (Italy). Begun 1294. *Plan and Interior* (Arnold V. Borsig, N.Y.)

255 Castel del Monte, Apulia (Italy). c. 1240. *View and Plan* (H. Decker, *Romanesque Art in Italy*, pl. 191)

256 Town Hall (Palazzo Pubblico), Siena (Italy). 1288–1309. *Façade* (Alinari)

page 256 City of Siena. 14th century. *Plan of Central Area* (W. Braunfels, *Mittelalterliche ... Toscana*, pl. IV)

257 Palazzo Vecchio, Florence (Italy). Begun 1298. *Exterior* (Alinari)

17. LATE GOTHIC ARCHITECTURE

258 Cathedral, Rouen (France). 13th–16th century. *West Façade* (Jeiter)

259 Abbey Church, St. Denis (France). 1231–81. *Interior* (Arch. Phot.)

260 Cathedral of Ste. Cécile, Albi (France). 1282–1390. *Exterior* (Roubier)

261 Cathedral of Ste. Cécile, Albi (France). 1282–1390. *Interior and Plan* (Arch. Phot.; E. Mâle, *La Cathédrale d'Albi*, p. 48)

262 Church of the Jacobins, Toulouse (France). 1294–1340. *Interior and Plan* (Rex, Toulouse)

263 Cathedral of Notre Dame, Sées (France). 1270–92. *Interior*

264 St. Maclou, Rouen (France). Begun 1434. *West Façade (1500–14), Interior, and Plan* (Giraudon; Arch. Phot.; Lasteyrie, I, pl. 213)

265 St. Séverin, Paris (France). 1489–91. *Choir* (Hurault)

266 House of Jacques Coeur, Bourges (France). 1443–51. *Courtyard and Plan* (Arch. Phot.; Lurçat, IV, p. 141)

267 Cathedral, Exeter (England). c. 1280–1370. *Interior* (Kersting)

268 Cathedral, Ely (England). 1323–c. 1330. *Interior of Octagon* (Felton)

269 Cathedral, Gloucester (England). 1332–77. *Interior* (Kersting)

270 Cathedral Cloister, Gloucester (England). 1357–77. *East Walk* (Felton)

271 Cathedral, Wells (England). 1338. *Arches of Crossing* (Kersting)

272 Chapel of King's College, Cambridge (England). 1446–1515. *Interior* (Kersting)

273 Chapel of King's College, Cambridge (England). 1446–1515. *Exterior and Plan* (Edwin Smith)

274 Church of the Holy Cross (Heiligkreuzkirche), Schwäbisch Gmünd (Germany). Begun 1351. *Interior and Plan* (DKV; H. Sedlmayr, *Deutsche Baukunst*)

275 St. Sebald, Nuremberg (Germany). 1361–72. *Interior* (SBB)

276 Matthäus Böblinger. *Münster Tower, Ulm.* Drawing, 1482. *Münsterbauamt, Ulm (Germany)*

276 Münster, Ulm (Germany). 1377–1492. *View of Tower* (SBB)

277 St. Anne, Annaberg (Germany). Begun 1499. *Interior and Plan* (Deutsche Fotothek; H. Sedlmayr, *Deutsche Baukunst*)

278 Town Hall, Münster (Germany). Mid-14th century. *Façade* (Marburg)

279 Benedict Rieth. Vladislav Hall, Castle, Prague (Czechoslovakia). 1487–1502. *Interior* (Schmidt-Glassner)

279 Burkard Engelberg. Münster, Ulm (Germany). Completed 1507. *Side Aisles* (Lala Aufsberg, Sonthofen)

280 Cathedral, Gerona (Spain). 1312–1549. *Interior and Plan* (Mas; P. Lavedan, *L'Architecture ... Baléares*)

281 S. Gregorio, Valladolid (Spain). 1488–96. *Upper Façade* (Mas)

282 Cathedral of S. Maria del Fiore, Florence (Italy). Begun 1296, by Arnolfo di Cambio; dome 1420–36, by Filippo Brunelleschi. *Interior and Plan* (Alinari)

283 Cathedral of S. Maria del Fiore, Florence (Italy). 1296–1436. *Exterior* (Alinari)

284 Filippo Brunelleschi. Dome of Cathedral, Florence (Italy). 1420–36. *Diagram showing Construction* (S. P. Sanpaolesi, "La cupola di S. M. del Fiore: il projetto, la costruzione," pl. VII)

285 Campanile, Cathedral, Florence (Italy). Designed by Giotto di Bondone; built 1334–59 (Alinari)

286 Lorenzo Maitani and others. Cathedral, Orvieto (Italy). c. 1310. *West Façade* (Anderson)

287 Cathedral, Milan (Italy). Begun 1386. *Exterior* (Fototeca Unione)

288 Cathedral, Milan (Italy). Begun 1386. *Interior and Plan* (Alinari; G. Franchetti, *Storia ... Milano*, pl. I)

289 Cathedral, Milan (Italy). Begun 1386. *Theoretical Section* (C. Cesariano, *Vitruvius De Architettura*, Como, 1521)

290 Ca' d'Oro, Venice (Italy). 1422–c. 1440. *Façade* (Alinari)

THE MIDDLE AGES

14. *Early Medieval Architecture*

Gatehouse, Monastery, Lorsch (Germany). 767–74. *View of Façade*

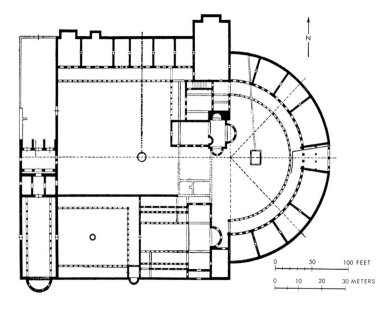

ABOVE
St. Riquier, Centula
(Picardy, France).
Consecrated 799.
*Engraving by Petau, 1612,
after an 11th-century
Manuscript Illustration*

LEFT
Palace of Charlemagne,
Ingelheim (Germany).
774–87. *Plan*

Palatine Chapel, Aachen (Germany). 792–805. *Façade from the west*

Palatine Chapel, Aachen (Germany). 792–805. *Interior View toward the east*

N

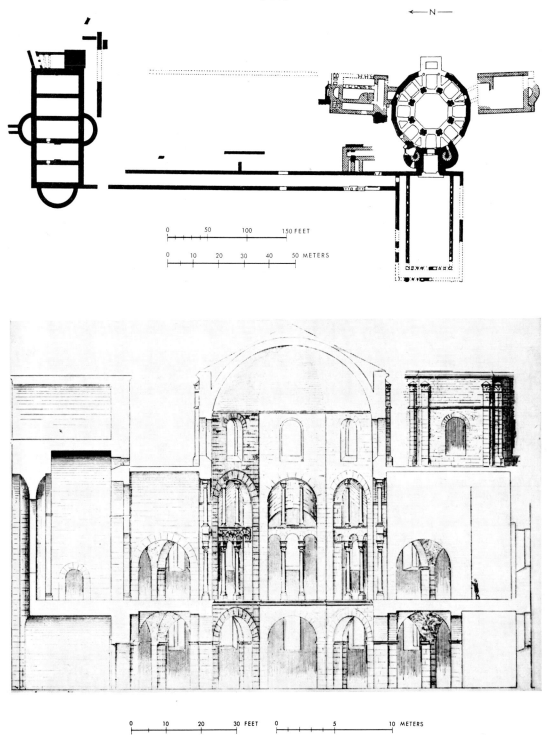

0   50   100   150 FEET

0   10   20   30   40   50 METERS

0   10   20   30 FEET   0   5   10 METERS

Palace of Charlemagne and Palatine Chapel, Aachen (Germany). c. 790–805.
General Plan, and Longitudinal Section of Chapel (restored)

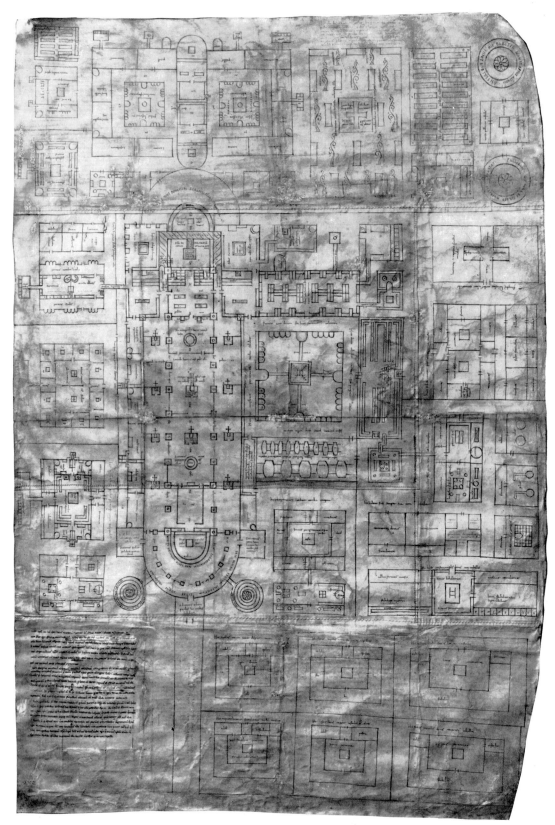

Plan for a Monastery. Ink on parchment, c. 820.
Chapter Library, St. Gall (Switzerland)

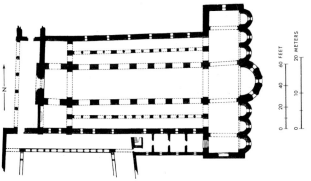

S. Maria, Ripoll (Catalonia, Spain). Nave, late 10th century; transept, 1018–32.
Exterior from southeast (after reconstruction), and Plan

St. Michael, Hildesheim (Germany). 1001–1033. *View of Interior toward the west
(photograph taken before World War II)*

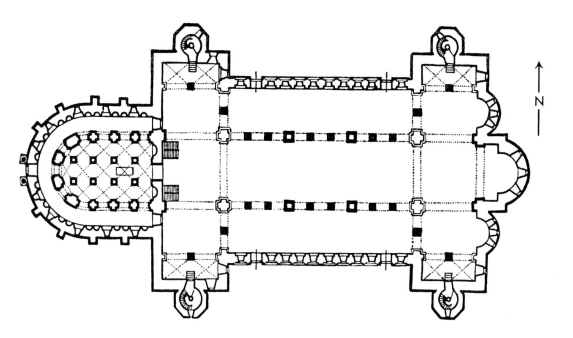

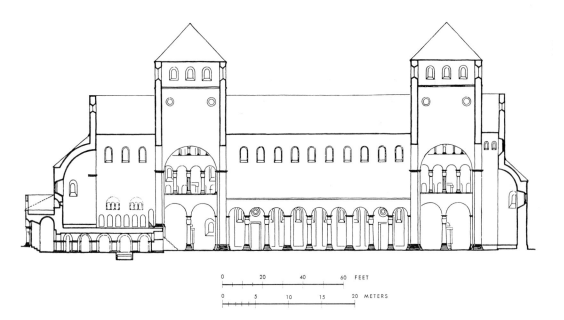

St. Michael, Hildesheim (Germany). 1001–1033.
Plan and Longitudinal Section (both reconstructed)

Ste. Gertrude, Nivelles (Belgium). 1000–1046. *View of Interior
toward Nave and Choir (after restoration), and Plan*

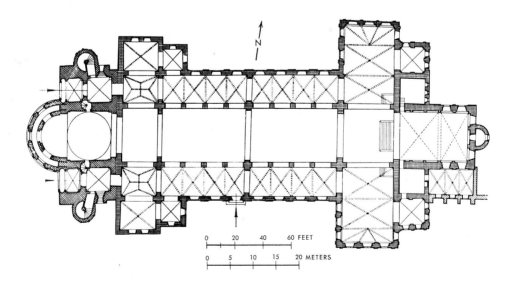

West Tower, Earl's Barton (Northamptonshire, England). c. 1000.
Exterior from southwest

THE MIDDLE AGES

15. Romanesque Architecture

Cathedral, Pisa (Italy). Begun 1063. *View of Interior toward the east*

RIGHT
Cathedral Square, Pisa (Italy). Cathedral, begun 1063;
Baptistery, 1153–1265; Campanile, begun 1174. *General Plan,
and View from southwest; Plan of Cathedral*

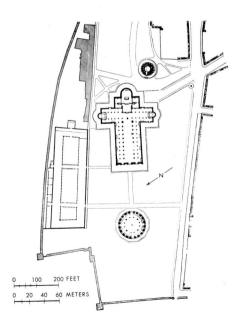

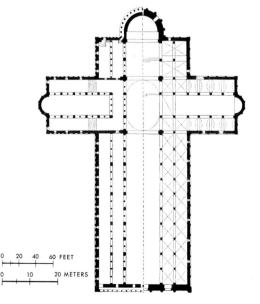

Basilica of St. Mark,
Venice (Italy). 1063–94.
West Façade

Basilica of St. Mark,
Venice (Italy). 1063–94.
Air View from the west

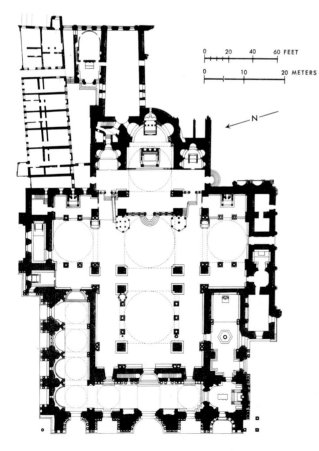

Basilica of St. Mark,
Venice (Italy).
1063–94. *View of Interior
toward the east, and Plan*

S. Ambrogio, Milan (Italy).
Late 11th–12th century.
*Interior and Exterior,
from the west*

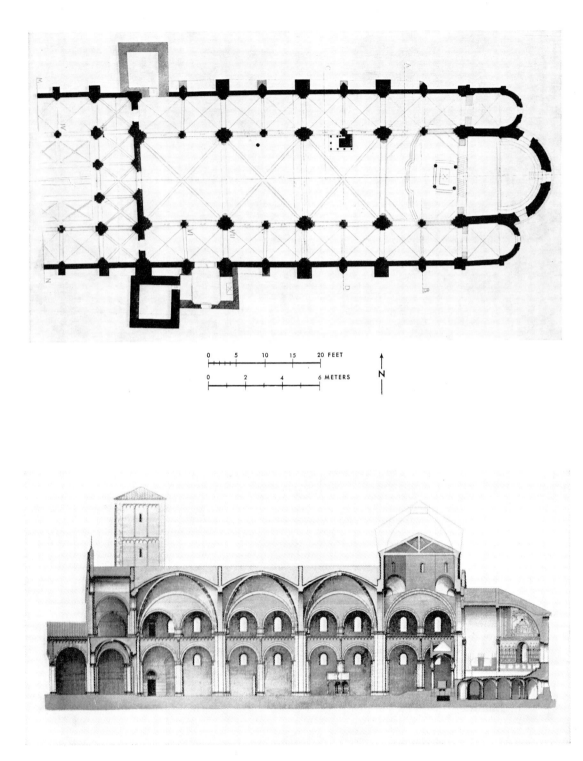

S. Ambrogio, Milan (Italy). Late 11th–12th century.
Plan and Longitudinal Section

Third Abbey Church and Monastery, Cluny (France). Church, 1088–c. 1121;
monastery, c. 1157. *View from northwest, in 1798 (portion of
watercolor painting by J.-B. Lallemand, Bibliothèque Nationale, Paris),
and Plan (reconstructed by K. J. Conant)*

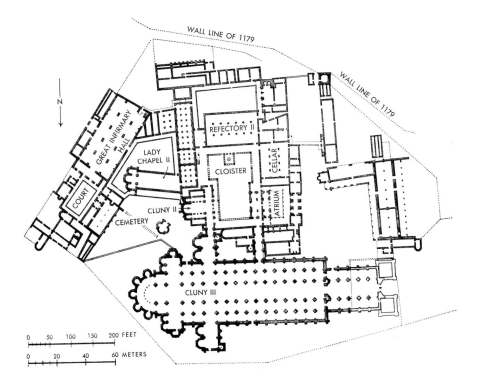

St. Étienne (Abbaye-aux-Hommes), Caen (France).
Begun c. 1068; towers 13th century. *West Façade*

St. Étienne
(Abbaye-aux-Hommes),
Caen (France).
Begun c. 1068;
vaulted c. 1115–20.
*View of Interior
toward the east,
and Plan*

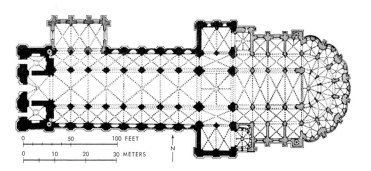

St. Philibert, Tournus (France). c. 960–1120. *View of Nave Arcade*

St. Philibert, Tournus (France). Ambulatory, 979–1019;
lantern, 1120. *Exterior View from southeast*

St. Savin sur Gartempe (France). Nave, c. 1095–1115;
choir, c. 1060–75. *View of Interior toward the east,
showing Frescoes in Nave Vault ("The Bible of St. Savin")*

Cathedral of St. Lazare, Autun (France). c. 1120–32.
North Wall of Nave, from Crossing

Notre Dame la Grande, Poitiers (France). c. 1130–45. *West Façade*

Cathedral of St. Front, Périgueux (France). c. 1125–50.
Air View from northeast

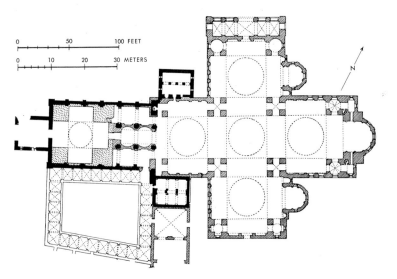

Cathedral of St. Front,
Périgueux (France).
c. 1125–50. *View of
Interior toward the east,
and Plan*

St. Sernin, Toulouse (France). c. 1080–1120.
View of Interior toward the east

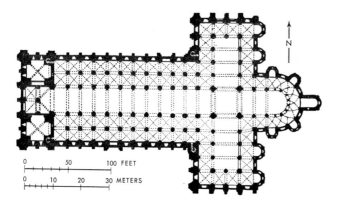

St. Sernin, Toulouse
(France). c. 1080–1120.
*Air View from
southeast, and Plan*

Cathedral, Winchester (England). c. 1090.
Interior View of North Transept from southeast

Cathedral, Durham (England). 1093–1133. *View of Interior toward the east*

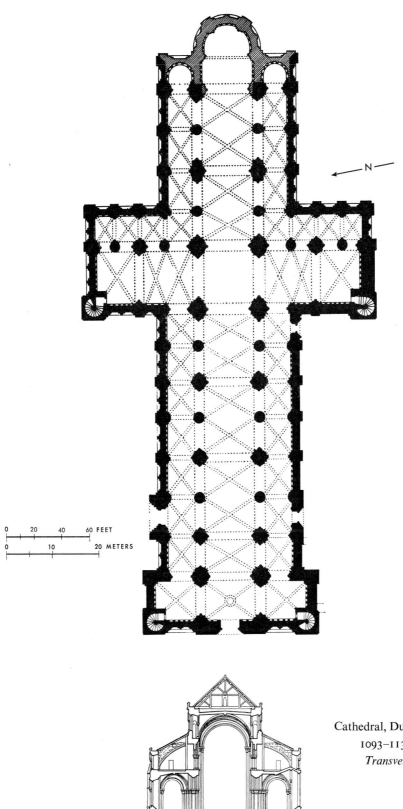

N

Cathedral, Durham (England).
1093–1133. *Plan and
Transverse Section*

St. Mary in Capitol, Cologne (Germany). c. 1030–after 1069.
View of Exterior from northeast

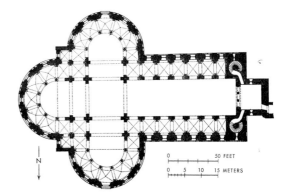

St. Mary in Capitol, Cologne
(Germany). c. 1030–after 1069.
*View of Interior (before
restoration) toward southeast,
and Plan*

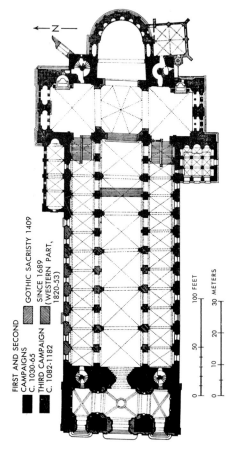

FIRST AND SECOND
CAMPAIGNS
C. 1030-65

GOTHIC SACRISTY 1409

THIRD CAMPAIGN
C. 1082-1182

SINCE 1689
(WESTERN PART,
1820-53)

100 FEET

50

30 METERS

20

10

Cathedral, Speyer (Germany). Begun 1030.
*Plan, and View of Interior toward the east
(early 19th-century engraving, before restoration)*

Cathedral,
Tournai (France).
Nave, 1110–71;
transept and crossing,
1165–1213. *Exterior
View from the north*

THE MIDDLE AGES

16. Gothic Architecture

Abbey Church, St. Denis (France). 1140–44.
Interior of Ambulatory (designed by Abbot Suger)

Abbey Church, St. Denis (France). 1140–44.
View of West Façade (early 19th-century engraving), and Plan

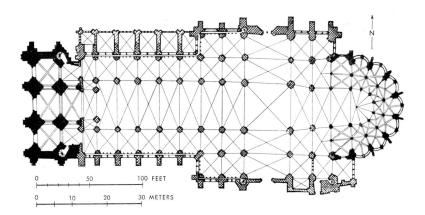

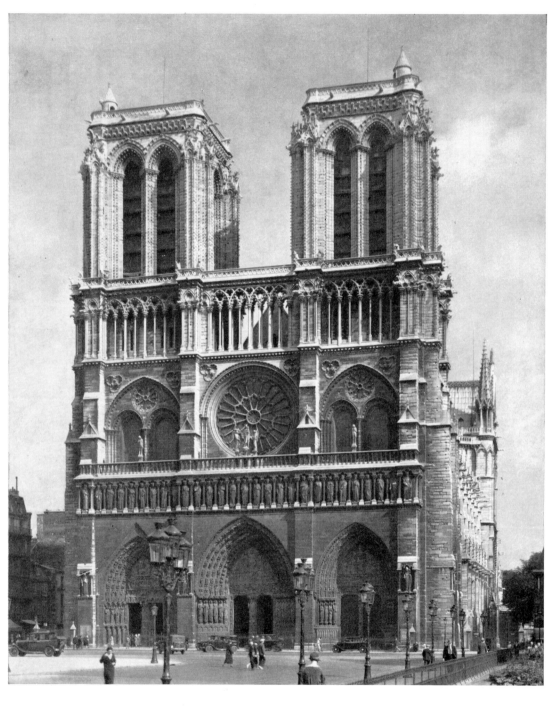

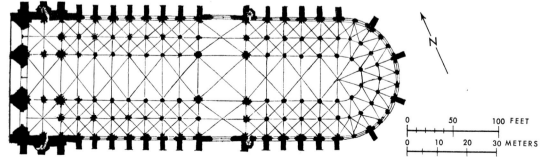

Cathedral of Notre Dame, Paris (France). 1163–c. 1250. *View of Interior toward the east (above), West Façade, and Plan (preceding page)*

Cathedral of Notre Dame,
Paris (France).
1163–c. 1250. *View of
Exterior from southeast*

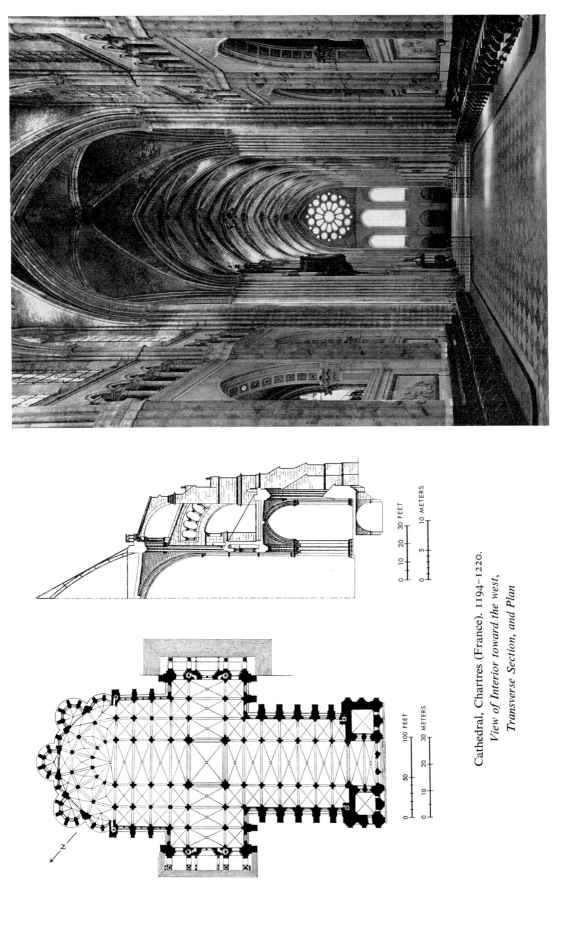

Cathedral, Chartres (France). 1194–1220.
View of Interior toward the west,
Transverse Section, and Plan

Cathedral,
Amiens (France).
*View into Vaults
of Choir*
(*1220–47*)

Cathedral, Amiens (France).
1220–88; façade, 1225–36;
towers, 1366–1420. *View of
Exterior from northwest*

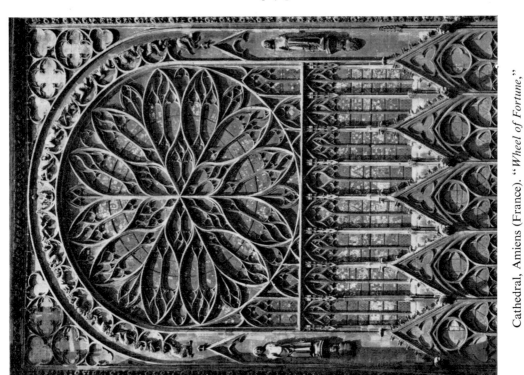

Cathedral, Amiens (France). "Wheel of Fortune,"
Rose Window in West Façade, completed 1269

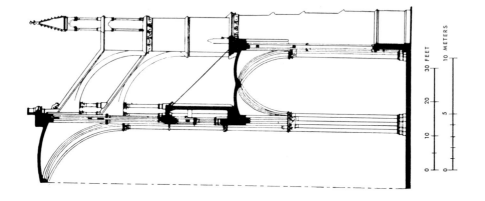

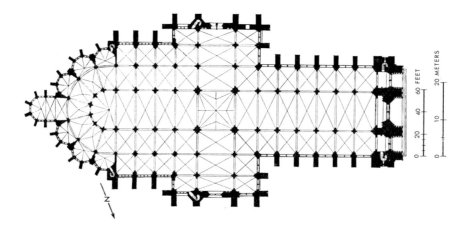

Cathedral, Amiens (France). 1220–88.
Plan and Transverse Section

Cathedral, Beauvais (France). Begun 1247.
Air View from southeast

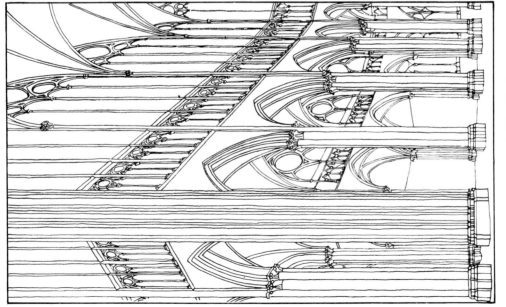

Cathedral, Beauvais (France). First Design, c. 1225.
Interior of Choir (reconstruction by Robert Branner)

Cathedral, Beauvais (France). Begun 1247. *View of Interior toward northeast*

Cathedral, Reims (France). c. 1225–99. *West Façade*

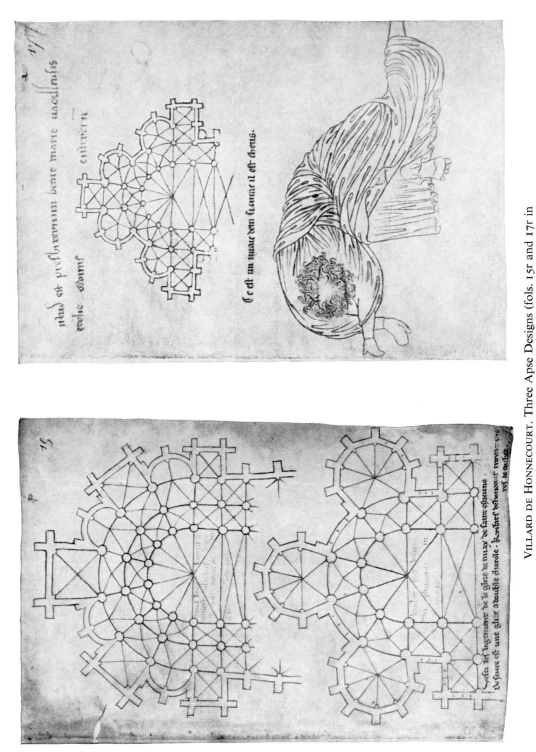

VILLARD DE HONNECOURT. Three Apse Designs (fols. 15r and 17r in *Sketchbook*, c. 1235). *Bibliothèque Nationale, Paris*

JAN VAN EYCK. *St. Barbara before a Gothic Tower.*
1437. Silverpoint on panel, 12 1/4 × 7 1/8″.
Royal Museum of Fine Arts, Antwerp

Pont St. Bénézet, Avignon (over Rhone River, France). 1177–85. *View from the west*

Ramparts (surrounding walls), Aigues-Mortes (France). 1240–72. *Outer View*

Cathedral, Salisbury (England). 1220–70. *View of Exterior from southeast*

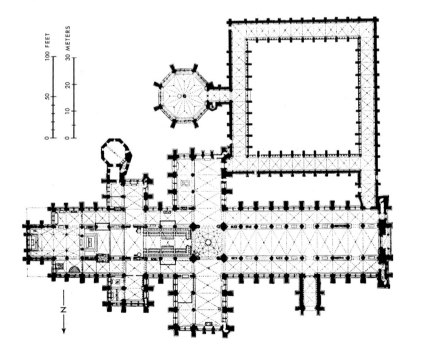

Cathedral, Salisbury (England). 1220–70.
View of Interior toward the east, and General Plan

Church of Our Lady (Liebfrauenkirche), Trier (Germany).
1235–c. 1253. *West Façade*

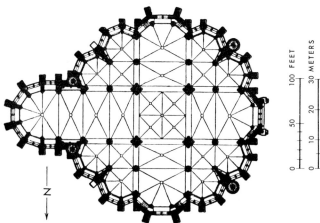

Church of Our Lady
(Liebfrauenkirche),
Trier (Germany).
1235–c. 1253.
*View of Interior
toward the east,
and Plan*

Abbey, Fossanova (Priverno, Italy). Consecrated 1208.
Exterior View of Church from northwest

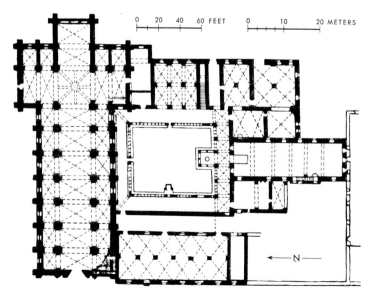

Abbey, Fossanova
(Priverno, Italy).
Consecrated 1208.
*Interior View of
Church toward the east,
and General Plan*

Cathedral, Siena (Italy). Completed c. 1264. *Interior View toward northeast, into Crossing*

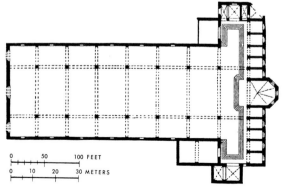

S. Croce, Florence (Italy).
Begun 1294. *Plan, and View of
Interior toward the east*

0   50   100 FEET
0 10 20 30 METERS

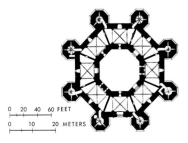

Castel del Monte, Apulia (Italy). c. 1240.
View of Entrance Doorway, and Plan

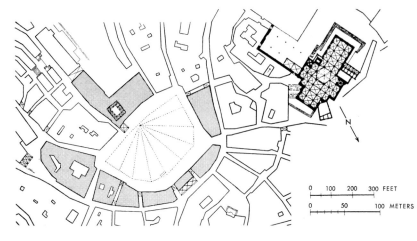

ABOVE
Town Hall
(Palazzo Pubblico),
Siena (Italy). 1288–1309.
Façade from the north

RIGHT
City of Siena.
14th century.
Plan of Central Area

0 100 200 300 FEET

0   50   100 METERS

Palazzo Vecchio, Florence (Italy). Begun 1298. *Exterior from northwest*

THE MIDDLE AGES

17. Late Gothic Architecture

Cathedral, Rouen (France). 13th–16th century. *West Façade*

Abbey Church, St. Denis (France). 1231–81. *View of Interior toward the east*

Cathedral of Ste. Cécile, Albi (France). 1282–1390 (porch 1520–35).
View of Exterior from the east

Cathedral of Ste. Cécile,
Albi (France). 1282–1390.
*View of Interior
toward the east, and Plan*

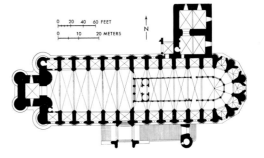

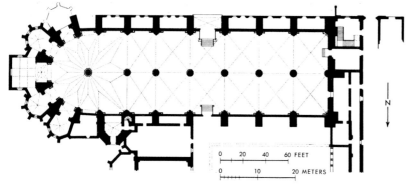

Church of the Jacobins,
Toulouse (France).
1294–1340. *View of
Interior toward
the east, and Plan*

Cathedral of Notre Dame, Sées (France). 1270–92.
View of Interior toward the east

St. Maclou, Rouen
(France). Begun 1434.
West Façade (1500–14),
Interior, and Plan

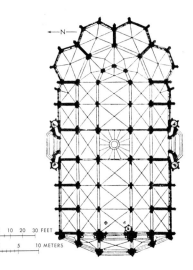

St. Séverin, Paris (France). 1489–91. *Interior View of Choir*

House of Jacques Coeur,
silversmith and merchant,
Bourges (France). 1443–51.
*View of Courtyard from
southeast, and Plan*

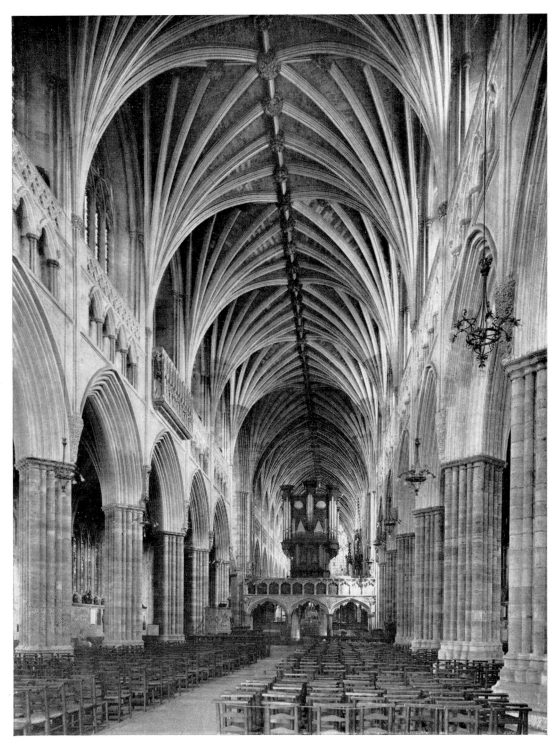

Cathedral, Exeter (England). c. 1280–1370. *View of Interior toward the east*

Cathedral, Ely (England). 1323–c. 1330. *View into Octagon over Crossing*

Cathedral, Gloucester (England). 1332–77. *Interior of Choir toward the east*

Cathedral Cloister, Gloucester (England). 1357–77. *Interior View of East Walk*

Cathedral, Wells (England). 1338. *Arches of the Crossing;*
View across Transepts toward the north

Chapel of King's College, Cambridge (England). 1446–1515. *View of
Interior toward the west, Exterior from the south, and Plan*

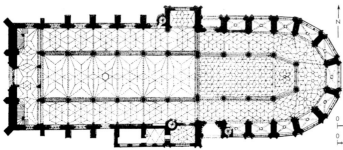

Church of the Holy Cross
(Heiligkreuzkirche),
Schwäbisch Gmünd
(Germany). Begun 1351.
*View of Interior
toward the east, and Plan*

St. Sebald, Nuremberg (Germany). 1361–72. *View of Interior toward the east*

MATTHÄUS BÖBLINGER. *Münster Tower,*
Ulm. Drawing, 1482.
Münsterbauamt, Ulm (Germany)

Münster, Ulm (Germany). 1377–1492. *Exterior*
from southwest (upper part of Tower
completed 1877–90, to original design)

St. Anne, Annaberg (Germany).
Begun 1499. *Interior View
toward the west, and Plan*

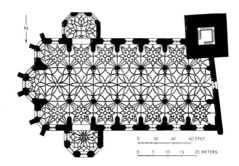

Town Hall, Münster (Germany). Mid-14th century. *Façade*

ABOVE
BENEDICT RIETH. Vladislav Hall,
Castle, Prague (Czechoslovakia).
1487–1502. *View of Interior*

LEFT
BURKARD ENGELBERG. Münster,
Ulm (Germany).
Completed 1507. *Interior of
Side Aisles toward the east*

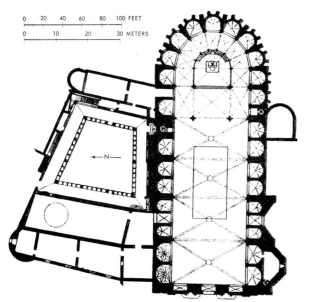

Cathedral, Gerona (Spain).
1312–1549; nave, 1417–1549;
chevet, 1312–46. *View of Interior
toward the east, and Plan*

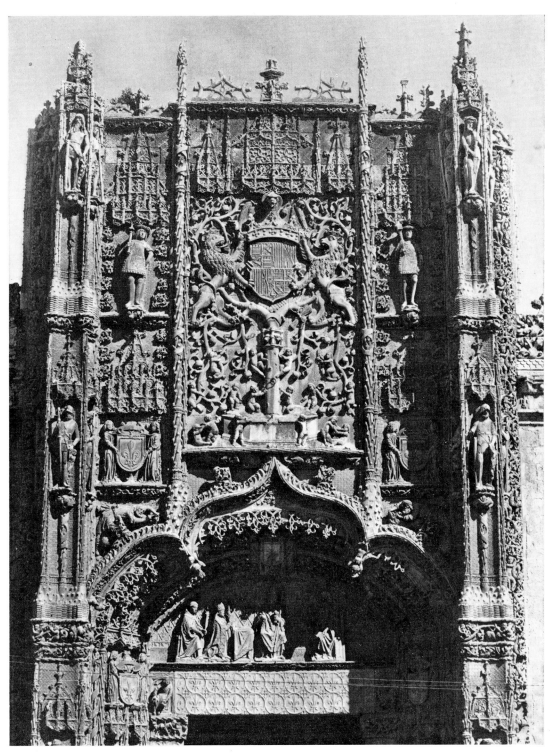

S. Gregorio, Valladolid (Spain). 1488–96. *Upper Portion of Façade*

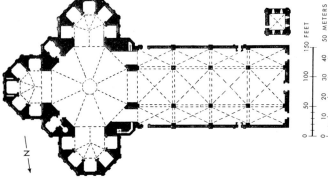

Cathedral of S. Maria
del Fiore, Florence
(Italy). Begun 1296,
by ARNOLFO DI CAMBIO;
dome 1420–36,
by FILIPPO BRUNELLESCHI.
*View of Interior toward
the east, and Plan*

Cathedral of S. Maria del Fiore, Florence (Italy). 1296–1436.
View of Exterior from southeast

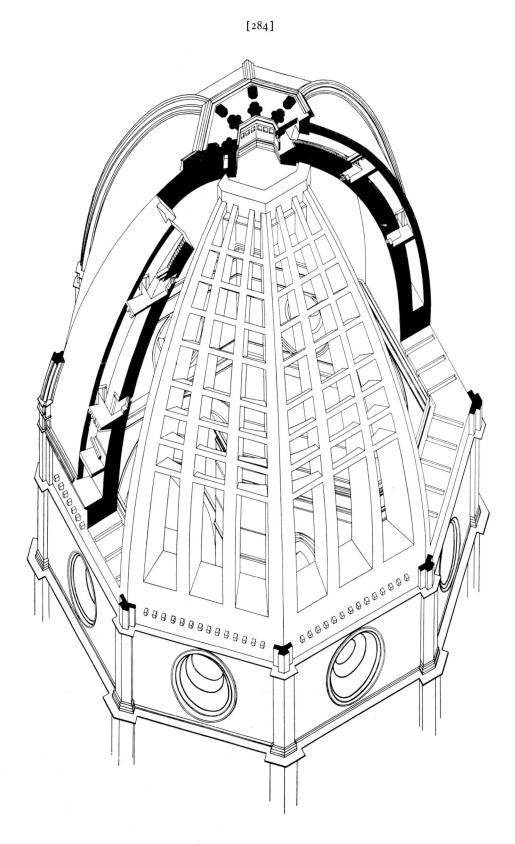

FILIPPO BRUNELLESCHI. Dome of Cathedral, Florence (Italy).
1420–36. *Diagram showing Construction*

Campanile, Cathedral,
Florence (Italy).
Designed by
GIOTTO DI BONDONE;
built 1334–59.
View from the east

LORENZO MAITANI and others. Cathedral, Orvieto (Italy). c. 1310. *West Façade*

Cathedral,
Milan (Italy).
Begun 1386.
*View of Exterior
from southwest*

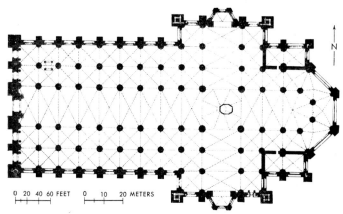

Cathedral, Milan (Italy).
Begun 1386. *View of
Interior toward the east,
and Plan*

0 20 40 60 FEET   0   10   20 METERS

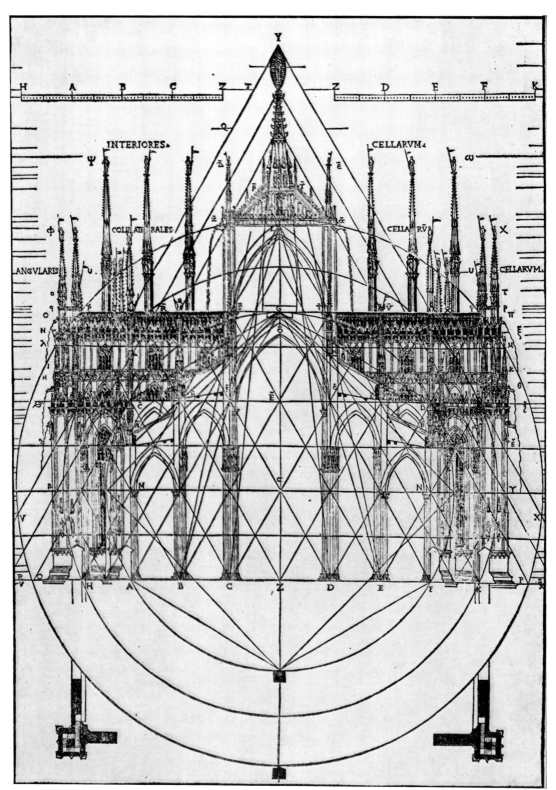

Cathedral, Milan (Italy). Begun 1386. *Theoretical Section, Derived from Equilateral Triangle*

Ca' d'Oro, Venice (Italy). 1422–c. 1440. *Façade from southwest*

THE RENAISSANCE

LIST OF ILLUSTRATIONS

18. EARLY RENAISSANCE ARCHITECTURE

page 301 FILIPPO BRUNELLESCHI. Foundling Hospital (Spedale degli Innocenti), Florence. Designed 1419. *Exterior* (Alinari)

302 FILIPPO BRUNELLESCHI. S. Lorenzo, Florence. Designed 1418. *Interior* (Anderson)

303 FILIPPO BRUNELLESCHI. S. Lorenzo, Florence. Designed 1418. *Plan, and Interior of Old Sacristy* (Anderson)

304 FILIPPO BRUNELLESCHI. Pazzi Chapel, S. Croce, Florence. c. 1430–46. *Interior* (Kidder Smith)

304 FILIPPO BRUNELLESCHI. Pazzi Chapel, S. Croce, Florence. c. 1430–46. *Façade* (Anderson)

305 FILIPPO BRUNELLESCHI. Pazzi Chapel, S. Croce, Florence. c. 1430–46. *Plan*

305 FILIPPO BRUNELLESCHI. S. Maria degli Angeli, Florence. Begun 1434. *Plan, and Drawing after Brunelleschi's Design* (Christian Huelsen, *Il Libro di Giuliano da Sangallo*, Vatican, 1910, fol. 15v; Biblioteca Laurenziana, Florence)

306 FILIPPO BRUNELLESCHI. S. Spirito, Florence. Designed 1436. *Plan and Interior* (Rollie McKenna)

307 MICHELOZZO DI BARTOLOMMEO. Palazzo Medici-Riccardi, Florence. 1444–60. *Exterior and Plan* (Alinari; Stegmann and Geymüller, vol. I, pl. 33)

308 MICHELOZZO DI BARTOLOMMEO. Palazzo Medici-Riccardi, Florence. 1444–60. *Courtyard* (Alinari)

309 LEONE BATTISTA ALBERTI. Palazzo Rucellai, Florence. 1446–51. *Façade* (Anderson)

310 LEONE BATTISTA ALBERTI. S. Francesco, Rimini. 1446–50. *Exterior* (Vincent)

311 BERNARDO ROSSELLINO. Piazza Pio II, Pienza. 1459–62. *Plan* (after E. Peets and W. Hegeman, *Civic Art*, p. 25)

312 Palazzo Venezia, Rome. 1465–71. *Façade and Plan* (Von Matt; after T. Magnuson, *Studies... Architecture*, pl. IV)

313 Palazzo Venezia, Rome. 1465–71. *Courtyard* (Anderson)

313 LEONE BATTISTA ALBERTI. S. Andrea, Mantua. Designed 1470. *Façade* (Rollie McKenna)

314 LEONE BATTISTA ALBERTI. S. Andrea, Mantua. Designed 1470. *Interior* (Alinari)

315 LEONE BATTISTA ALBERTI. S. Andrea, Mantua. Designed 1470. *Interior and Plan* (Rollie McKenna)

316 GIULIANO DA SANGALLO. Villa Medici, Poggio a Cajano. c. 1480. *Façade and Plan* (Alinari; Stegmann and Geymüller, vol. I, p. 120)

317 FRANCESCO DI GIORGIO. *Anthropomorphic Derivations of Church Plan and Church Façade.* c. 1490–95. *Biblioteca Nazionale, Florence*

317 GIULIANO DA SANGALLO. S. Maria delle Carceri, Prato. 1485–92. *Exterior* (Alinari)

318 GIULIANO DA SANGALLO. S. Maria delle Carceri, Prato. 1485–92. *Interior and Plan* (Alinari; Bibl. Com., Siena)

319 DONATO BRAMANTE. S. Maria presso S. Satiro, Milan. c. 1480. *Interior and Plan* (Aragozzini; O. Foerstor, *Bramante*, p. 91)

320 LEONARDO DA VINCI. *Project for a Church.* c. 1490. (Giraudon)

320 DONATO BRAMANTE. S. Maria delle Grazie, Milan. Begun 1492. *Exterior* (Aragozzini)

321 DONATO BRAMANTE. S. Maria delle Grazie, Milan. Begun 1492. *Interior and Plan* (Aragozzini; H. Strack, *Central... in Italien*, pl. 11, fig. 19)

322 MAURO CODUCCI. S. Zaccaria, Venice. c. 1483–1500. *Façade* (Fiorentini)

19. HIGH RENAISSANCE ARCHITECTURE

page 323 DONATO BRAMANTE. S. Maria della Pace, Rome. 1504. *Cloister* (Anderson)

324 DONATO BRAMANTE. Tempietto, S. Pietro in Montorio, Rome. 1504. *Exterior and Plan* (G. F. N.)

325 DONATO BRAMANTE. Belvedere Court, Vatican City (Rome). Begun 1503. *North Façade and General View* (Arch. Foto. Vaticano; Sopr. Gal. Flor.)

326 DONATO BRAMANTE. Basilica of St. Peter, Vatican City (Rome). c. 1508. *Plan* (Sopr. Gal. Flor.)

327 Basilica of St. Peter, Vatican City. First Plan by DONATO BRAMANTE. 1506. (Sopr. Gal. Flor.)

327 Basilica of St. Peter. Exterior Design by DONATO BRAMANTE. 1506. *Medal by Caradosso (British Museum, London)*

327 Basilica of St. Peter. Plan by RAPHAEL. 1514–20.

328 S. Maria della Consolazione, Todi. Begun 1508. *Exterior* (G. F. N.)

329 S. Maria della Consolazione, Todi. Begun 1508. *Interior* (Alinari)

330 S. Maria della Consolazione, Todi. Begun 1508. *Plan and Section* (Laspeyres, *S. Maria... Todi*, pl. I; Pollitzer)

331 RAPHAEL. S. Eligio degli Orefici, Rome. Begun 1509. *Dome and Plan* (Neuerburg; after Geymüller, *Raffaello Sanzio...*, fig. 5)

331 DONATO BRAMANTE. Palazzo dei Tribunali, Rome. c. 1512. *Plan* (Sopr. Gal. Flor.)

332 DONATO BRAMANTE. Palazzo Caprini-Raphael, Rome. c. 1514. *Façade* (Pollitzer)

332 RAPHAEL. Palazzo Vidoni-Caffarelli, Rome. c. 1515–20. *Exterior* (Anderson)

20. SIXTEENTH-CENTURY ARCHITECTURE IN ITALY

333 ANTONIO DA SANGALLO and MICHELANGELO. Palazzo Farnese, Rome. 1530–89. *Façade* (Alinari)

334 ANTONIO DA SANGALLO and MICHELANGELO. Palazzo Farnese, Rome. 1530–89. *Plan and Section* (Letarouilly, *Les Édifices...*, vol. II, pls. 116 and 125)

335 ANTONIO DA SANGALLO and MICHELANGELO. Palazzo Farnese, Rome. 1530–89. *Courtyard* (Anderson)

335 ANTONIO DA SANGALLO. Piazza Farnese, Rome. 1535–50. *General Plan* (Quaroni)

336 MICHELANGELO. Laurentian Library, Florence. 1524. *Entry Hall and Staircase* (Alinari)

336 GIULIO ROMANO. Palazzo del Tè, Mantua. 1525–35. *Portion of Courtyard* (G. F. N.)

337 JACOPO SANSOVINO. Library of St. Mark, Venice. Begun 1536. *Exterior* (Anderson)

338 BALDASSARE PERUZZI. Palazzo Massimi, Rome. Begun 1535. *Façade* (Alinari)

338 MICHELANGELO. Palazzo dei Conservatori, The Capitol, Rome. 1538–61. *Exterior* (Fototeca Unione)

339 MICHELANGELO. The Capitol, Rome. Designed 1537. *View (Dupérac), and Plan* (G. N. S.; Letarouilly, *Les Édifices...*, vol. II)

340 PIRRO LIGORIO. Villa d'Este, Tivoli. Designed 1549. *View (Dupérac)* (D. Coffin, *Villa d'Este...*, pl. I)

341 GIORGIO VASARI, GIACOMO VIGNOLA, and BARTOLOMMEO AMMANATI. Villa Giulia, Rome. 1550–55. *Garden Façade, Section, and Plan* (Alinari; Letarouilly, *Les Édifices...*, vol. II)

342 GIORGIO VASARI. Uffizi Palace, Florence. Begun 1560. *Exterior and Loggia* (Alinari; Hilda Lotz)

343 MICHELANGELO. Basilica of St. Peter, Vatican City. 1546–64. *Exterior and Plan* (Fototeca Unione)

344 MICHELANGELO. Basilica of St. Peter, Vatican City. 1546–64. *Section and Interior* (Pollitzer; Degenhart)

345 GUIDO GUIDETTI. S. Caterina dei Funari, Rome. Begun 1564. *Façade* (Anderson)

346 ANDREA PALLADIO. Villa Rotonda, Vicenza. Begun 1550. *Exterior, Plan, and Section* (Rollie McKenna; Ware, *Palladio*, pl. XIII)

347 ANDREA PALLADIO. S. Giorgio Maggiore, Venice. Designed 1565. *Façade* (Fond. Cini)

348 ANDREA PALLADIO. S. Giorgio Maggiore, Venice. Designed 1565. *Interior and Plan* (Fond. Cini)

349 ANDREA PALLADIO. Teatro Olimpico, Vicenza. 1580–84. *Stage* (Vajenti)

page 350 GIACOMO VIGNOLA and GIACOMO DELLA PORTA. Church of the Gesù, Rome. c. 1575–84. *Interior* (Anderson)

351 GIACOMO VIGNOLA and GIACOMO DELLA PORTA. Church of the Gesù, Rome. c. 1575–84. *Plan and Façade* (Vincent)

352 ANDREA SACCHI and JAN MIEL. *Pope Urban VIII Visiting Il Gesù.* 1639–41. *National Gallery, Rome* (G. F. N.)

353 DOMENICO FONTANA and POPE SIXTUS V. *Plan for Rome.* 1585–90 (Giedion, *Space, Time and Architecture*, fig. 27)

354 VINCENZO SCAMOZZI. City of Palmanova (Veneto). 1593. *Air View* (Aerofilms)

21. SIXTEENTH-CENTURY ARCHITECTURE OUTSIDE ITALY

355 Château of Blois (France). 1515–24. *Spiral Staircase in Courtyard* (Schmidt-Glassner)

356 DOMENICO DA CORTONA (?). Château of Chambord (France). *Exterior* (Arch. Phot.)

357 DOMENICO DA CORTONA (?). Château of Chambord (France). Begun 1519. *Plan and Staircase* (Ducerceau, *Les plus excellents bastiments;* Schmidt-Glassner)

358 GILLES LE BRETON. Château of Fontainebleau (France). Begun 1528. *Stairs, by Jean Ducerceau, in Cour du Cheval Blanc* (Roubier)

359 GILLES LE BRETON and PHILIBERT DE L'ORME. Château of Fontainebleau (France). 1540–56. *Ballroom* (Marburg)

360 HECTOR SOHIER. St. Pierre, Caen (France). 1528–45. *Exterior* (Marburg)

361 PHILIBERT DE L'ORME. Château of Anet (France). Frontispiece (before 1550). *Reerected in courtyard of École des Beaux-Arts, Paris* (Courtauld Inst.)

361 PHILIBERT DE L'ORME. Château of Anet (France). 1552. *Main Gate* (Roubier)

362 PIERRE LESCOT. The Louvre, Paris. *Façade (begun 1546), and Air View* (Giraudon; C. A. F.)

363 PEDRO MACHUCA. Palace of Charles V, Granada (Spain). Begun 1527. *Courtyard and Plan* (Mas; after Chueca)

364 DIEGO DA SILOE. Cathedral, Granada (Spain). Begun 1529. *Interior and Plan* (Mas; E.E. Rosenthal, *The Cathedral of Granada*, fig. 3)

365 JUAN DE HERRERA and JUAN BAUTISTA DE TOLEDO. Escorial (near Madrid, Spain). 1563–82. *Exterior and Plan* (Anderson)

366 JUAN DE HERRERA and JUAN BAUTISTA DE TOLEDO. Church, Escorial (near Madrid, Spain). 1572–85. *Interior at Crossing* (Mas)

366 DIOGO DE TORRALVA. Cristo Monastery, Tomar (Portugal). 1557–62. *Main Courtyard* (YAN)

367 FRANCISCO BECERRA. Cathedral, Cuzco (Peru). 1582–1654. *Interior* (Guillèn)

368 WOLFGANG MILLER and FRIEDRICH SUSTRIS. St. Michael, Munich (Germany). 1582–97. *Interior and Plan* (Schlegel; O. Hoever, *Vergleichende Architecturgeschichte*, fig. 129)

369 ELIAS HOLL. Town Hall, Augsburg (Germany). 1610–20. *Rear Façade* (Keetman)

370 ELIAS HOLL. Town Hall, Augsburg (Germany). *Golden Hall, 1615–20* (Kunstsammlungen Augsburg)

371 Wollaton Hall, Nottinghamshire (England). 1580–88. *Exterior* (© Country Life)

372 Burghley House, Northamptonshire (England). 1585. *Courtyard* (Kersting)

22. ARCHITECTURE OF THE SEVENTEENTH CENTURY IN ITALY

373 CARLO MADERNO. S. Susanna, Rome. 1597–1603. *Façade* (Anderson)

374 CARLO MADERNO. Basilica of St. Peter, Vatican City. 1606–12. *Main Façade* (Alinari)

375 CARLO MADERNO. Basilica of St. Peter, Vatican City. 1606–12. *Nave* (Alinari)

376 Basilica of St. Peter, Vatican City. *Interior, showing Tabernacle* (Kidder Smith)

376 Basilica of St. Peter, Vatican City. *Plan, showing Additions by* CARLO MADERNO, *1606–12* (Letarouilly, *Le Vatican...*, vol. I, pl. 39)

377 BALDASSARE LONGHENA. S. Maria della Salute, Venice. Begun 1631. *Exterior and Plan* (Kidder Smith)

page 378 PIETRO DA CORTONA. SS. Martina e Luca, Rome. 1635–50. *Façade and Plan* (Alinari; Fokker, pl. 105)

379 PIETRO DA CORTONA. SS. Martina e Luca, Rome. 1635–50. *Interior* (G. F. N.)

380 FRANCESCO BORROMINI. S. Carlo alle Quattro Fontane, Rome. Begun 1635. *View into Dome and Plan* (Alinari)

381 FRANCESCO BORROMINI. S. Carlo alle Quattro Fontane, Rome. *Façade* (Anderson)

382 FRANCESCO BORROMINI. S. Ivo della Sapienza, Rome. 1642–50. *Plan by Borromini, and Section* (Albertina, Vienna)

383 FRANCESCO BORROMINI. S. Ivo della Sapienza, Rome. 1642–50. *View* (Kidder Smith)

384 FRANCESCO BORROMINI and CARLO RAINALDI. S. Agnese in Piazza Navona, Rome. Begun 1652. *Façade and Plan* (Andrews; de' Rossi, *Insignium Roma Templorum*)

385 PIETRO DA CORTONA. S. Maria della Pace, Rome. 1656–57. *Façade and Plan* (Vincent)

386 Basilica of St. Peter, Vatican City. *Air View* (Fotocielo)

386 GIANLORENZO BERNINI. Basilica of St. Peter, Vatican City. *Colonnades* (Kersting)

387 GIANLORENZO BERNINI. S. Andrea al Quirinale, Rome. 1658–70. *Façade, Interior, and Plan* (List; Marburg; de' Rossi, *Insignium Roma Templorum*)

388 GIANLORENZO BERNINI. Palazzo Chigi-Odescalchi, Rome. Begun 1664. *Exterior* (Alinari)

389 GUARINO GUARINI. S. Lorenzo, Turin. 1666–79. *View into Dome, and Plan* (Sopr. Mon. Piemonte; Guarini, *Architettura Civile*, pl. 4)

390 GUARINO GUARINI. Chapel of the Holy Shroud, Cathedral, Turin. 1667–94. *Exterior View, and View into Dome* (Kidder Smith; Kidder Smith)

391 GUARINO GUARINI. Palazzo Carignano, Turin. 1679–92. *Exterior and Plan* (Kidder Smith; Millon)

392 GUARINO GUARINI. Palazzo Carignano, Turin. 1679–92. *Staircase* (Sopr. Mon. Piemonte)

23. SEVENTEENTH-CENTURY ARCHITECTURE IN FRANCE AND ENGLAND

393 Place des Vosges, Paris. Begun 1605. *Air View* (Herrard)

394 SALOMON DE BROSSE (?). St. Gervais, Paris. 1616. *Façade* (Marburg)

395 FRANÇOIS MANSART and JACQUES LEMERCIER. Church of the Val-de-Grâce, Paris. 1645–62. *Exterior and Plan* (Arch. Phot.)

396 FRANÇOIS MANSART and JACQUES LEMERCIER, Church of the Val-de-Grâce, Paris. 1645–62. *Interior* (Arch. Phot.)

397 FRANÇOIS MANSART. Château of Maisons (near Paris). 1642–46. *Entrance Court and Vestibule* (Andrews; Marburg)

398 LOUIS LE VAU. Château of Vaux-le-Vicomte (near Melun). 1657–61. *Exterior and Plan* (Andrews)

399 GIANLORENZO BERNINI. *Second Design for the Louvre, Paris* (Royal Museum, Stockholm)

399 LOUIS LE VAU. Château of Versailles. Begun 1669. *Garden Façade* (*Chalcographie du Louvre*, vol. XXII, pl. 61; Pollitzer)

400 LOUIS LE VAU and JULES HARDOUIN-MANSART. Château of Versailles. 1669–85. *Garden Façade* (Vizzavona)

401 LOUIS LE VAU and JULES HARDOUIN-MANSART. Château of Versailles. 1669–85. *Air View and Hall of Mirrors* (C.A.F.; Jean-Marie Marcel)

402 JULES HARDOUIN-MANSART, CHARLES LEBRUN, and ANTOINE COYSEVOX. Salon de la Guerre, Château of Versailles. Begun 1678. *Interior* (Vizzavona)

403 Tuileries Gardens, Paris. Mid-16th century. *Plan* (Ducerceau)

403 ANDRÉ LE NÔTRE. Tuileries Gardens, Paris. 1664–72. *Plan* (Blondel)

404 ANDRÉ LE NÔTRE. Château of Versailles. Begun 1667. *Plan of Gardens* (Arch. Phot.)

405 CLAUDE PERRAULT. East Façade of the Louvre, Paris. 1667–70 (Kersting)

406 JULES HARDOUIN-MANSART. Church of the Invalides, Paris. 1680–91. *Plan, Section, and Exterior* (Roubier; Blondel)

407 JULES HARDOUIN-MANSART. Place Vendôme, Paris. 1698. *Air View* (Herrard)

408 INIGO JONES. Banqueting House, Whitehall Palace, London. 1619–22. *West Façade* (RCHM)

409 SIR CHRISTOPHER WREN. Hampton Court Palace. Designed 1689. *Exterior* (RCHM)

page 409 SIR CHRISTOPHER WREN. Cathedral of St. Paul, London. 1675–1710. *West Façade* (NBR)

410 SIR CHRISTOPHER WREN. Cathedral of St. Paul, London. 1675–1710. *Interior and Plan* (A. Stratton, *Life... Wren*, p. 33; Edwin Smith)

411 SIR CHRISTOPHER WREN. *Plan for the Rebuilding of London after the Great Fire of 1666* (Courtauld Inst.)

24. SEVENTEENTH-CENTURY ARCHITECTURE IN FLANDERS, HOLLAND, SPAIN, GERMANY, AUSTRIA, AND THE NEW WORLD

412 FRANCESCO CARATTI. Czernin Palace, Prague (Czechoslovakia). Begun 1667. *Façade* (Schmidt-Glassner)

413 ANDREAS SCHLUETER. Royal Palace, Berlin (Germany). 1698–1706. *South Façade* (Schmidt-Glassner)

414 JOHANN LUKAS VON HILDEBRANDT. St. Lawrence, Gabel (Czechoslovakia). Begun 1699. *Exterior* (Statni ustav pamatkova Péce a Ochrany Prirody, Prague)

415 JOHANN LUKAS VON HILDEBRANDT. St. Lawrence, Gabel (Czechoslovakia). Begun 1699. *Interior, Plan, and Section* (Statni ustav pamatkova Péce a Ochrany Prirody, Prague)

416 JOHANN FISCHER VON ERLACH. Schloss Frain (Moravia, Czechoslovakia). 1689–95. *Exterior and Interior* (B. O. N.; Statni pamatkova sprava, Prague)

417 JOHANN FISCHER VON ERLACH. Schloss Frain (Moravia, Czechoslovakia). 1689–95. *Plan* (Sedlmeyr, *J. B. Fischer von Erlach;* Pollitzer)

417 JOHANN FISCHER VON ERLACH. Church of the Holy Trinity, Salzburg (Austria). 1694–1702. *Façade* (B. O. N.)

418 JOHANN FISCHER VON ERLACH. Church of the Holy Trinity, Salzburg (Austria). 1694–1702. *Interior of Church and Drawing of Complex* (Sedlmeyr, *J. B. Fischer von Erlach;* Pollitzer; Dr. Eva Frodl-Kraft, Vienna)

419 WILLIAM HESIUS. St. Michel, Louvain (Belgium). 1650. *Façade* (A. C. L.)

420 JACOB VAN CAMPEN and PIETER POST. Mauritshuis, The Hague (Holland). 1633. *Canal Façade* (© Fndn. Johan Maurits van Nassau, The Hague)

421 La Merced, Cuzco (Peru). 1651–69. *Cloister* (Guillèn)

421 Cathedral, Cuzco (Peru). 1651–54. *Central Portal* (Guillèn)

25. EIGHTEENTH-CENTURY ARCHITECTURE IN EUROPE AND THE NEW WORLD

422 NICOLA SALVI. Trevi Fountain, Rome (Italy). 1732–36. *View* (Anderson)

423 ALESSANDRO SPECCHI. Porta di Ripetta, Rome (Italy). Built 1703. *View* (courtesy Institute of Fine Arts, N. Y.)

423 FILIPPO JUVARRA. Superga, Turin (Italy). 1717–31. *Exterior* (Anderson)

424 FILIPPO JUVARRA. Royal Hunting Palace, Stupinigi (near Turin, Italy). 1729–33. *Interior* (Alinari)

425 FILIPPO JUVARRA. Royal Hunting Palace, Stupinigi (near Turin, Italy). 1729–33. *Air View and Exterior* (Moncalvo; Alinari)

426 FILIPPO JUVARRA. Church of the Carmine, Turin (Italy). 1732–35. *Interior* (Pedrini)

427 FERDINANDO FUGA. S. Maria Maggiore, Rome (Italy). 1741–43. *Façade* (Alinari)

427 ALESSANDRO GALILEI. S. Giovanni in Laterano, Rome (Italy). 1733–36. *Central Portion of East Façade* (Alinari)

428 PIETRO PASSALACQUA and DOMENICO GREGORINI. S. Croce in Gerusalemme, Rome (Italy). 1743. *Façade* (Alinari)

428 FRANCESCO DE SANCTIS. Spanish Steps, Rome (Italy). 1723–25 (Alinari)

429 FILIPPO RAGUZZINI. Piazza S. Ignazio, Rome (Italy). 1727–28. *View and Plan* (Alinari; Fokker, p. 245)

430 FERDINANDO FUGA. Palazzo della Consulta, Rome (Italy). 1732–37. *Façade* (Anderson)

430 GABRIELI VALVASSORI. Palazzo Doria-Pamphili, Rome (Italy). 1731–34. *Portion of Façade* (Alinari)

page 431 GABRIELI VALVASSORI. Palazzo Doria-Pamphili, Rome (Italy). 1731–34. *Main Gallery* (Masson)

432 GIOVANNI BATTISTA PIRANESI. S. Maria del Priorato, Rome (Italy). 1765. *Façade* (Fototeca Unione)

432 LUIGI VANVITELLI. Royal Palace, Caserta (Italy). 1752–74. *Main Staircase* (Masson)

433 LUIGI VANVITELLI. Royal Palace, Caserta (Italy). 1752–74. *Main Façade and Plan* (Masson)

434 BERNARDO VITTONE. S. Chiara, Brà (Italy). Begun 1742. *Exterior, Plan, and Section* (Moncalvo)

435 BERNARDO VITTONE. S. Chiara, Brà (Italy). Begun 1742. *Upper Interior* (Moncalvo)

436 JUSTE AURÈLE MEISSONIER. St. Sulpice, Paris (France). *Design for Façade* (Giraudon)

436 JEAN NICOLAS SERVANDONI. St. Sulpice, Paris (France). 1733. *Façade* (Marburg)

437 GERMAIN BOFFRAND. Hôtel de Soubise, Paris (France). Begun 1732. *Salon de la Princesse* (Andrews)

438 EMMANUEL HÉRÉ DE CORNY. Place de la Carrière and Hemicycle, Nancy (France). 1751–59. *Air View and Plan* (Enaud, *Cités de France;* Patte, pl. XXIV)

439 JACQUES ANGE GABRIEL. Petit Trianon, Versailles (France). 1762–64. *Garden Façade and Plan* (Arch. Phot.)

440 JACQUES GERMAIN SOUFFLOT. The Panthéon (Ste. Geneviève), Paris (France). 1755–92. *Interior and Plan* (Kersting)

441 RICHARD MIQUE. Le Hameau, Versailles (France). 1783. *Exterior*

442 JAMES GIBBS. St. Martin-in-the-Fields, London (England). 1721–26. *Façade* (Raymond R. Buckley)

442 JOHN WOOD THE ELDER and JOHN WOOD THE YOUNGER. The Circus and the Royal Crescent, Bath (England). c. 1754–75. *Air View* (Aerofilms)

443 ROBERT ADAM. Home House, London (England). 1772–73. *Front Drawing Room* (© Country Life)

443 ROBERT ADAM. House in the Adelphi, London (England). 1768–72. *Façade* (Gernsheim)

444 RICHARD BOYLE, EARL OF BURLINGTON, and WILLIAM KENT. Chiswick House, Chiswick (near London, England). Begun 1725. *Façade and Plan* (MW)

445 SIR JOHN VANBRUGH. Blenheim Palace, Woodstock (England). Begun 1705. *Garden Façade and Entrance Façade* (© Country Life; Edwin Smith)

446 SIR JOHN VANBRUGH. Blenheim Palace, Woodstock (England). Begun 1705. *Plan* (Campbell, *Vitruvius Britannicus*, vol. I, pl. 62)

446 Strawberry Hill, Twickenham (England). Enlarged 1750–70, by HORACE WALPOLE. *Holbein Chamber* (© Country Life)

447 JAKOB PRANDTAUER. Benedictine Abbey, Melk (Austria). Begun 1702. *General View* (Schmidt-Glassner)

448 JAKOB PRANDTAUER. Benedictine Abbey, Melk (Austria). 1702–c. 1738. *Plans and Interior* (Marburg)

449 JOHANN FISCHER VON ERLACH. St. Charles Borromaeus, Vienna (Austria). 1716–37. *Façade and Plan* (Schmidt-Glassner)

450 JOHANN FISCHER VON ERLACH. St. Charles Borromaeus, Vienna (Austria). 1716–37. *Interior* (K. P. V. Neubacher)

451 JOHANN LUKAS VON HILDEBRANDT. Upper Palace, Belvedere, Vienna (Austria). 1721–24. *Garden Façade and Interior* (Andrews; Schmidt-Glassner)

452 MATTHÄUS DANIEL PÖPPELMANN. The Zwinger, Dresden (Germany). 1711–22. *Exterior* (Renger-Patzsch)

453 COSMAS DAMIAN ASAM and EGID QUIRIN ASAM. Abbey Church, Rohr (Bavaria, Germany). 1717–21. *High Altar* (Marburg)

454 BALTHASAR NEUMANN. Episcopal Palace, Würzburg (Germany). 1719–44. *Interior of Kaisersaal* (DKV)

455 BALTHASAR NEUMANN. Episcopal Palace, Würzburg (Germany). 1719–44. *Central Staircase* (Müller)

456 JOHANN MICHAEL FISCHER. Benedictine Abbey, Ottobeuren (Germany). Begun 1744. *Exterior and Plan* (Toni Schneiders)

457 JOHANN MICHAEL FISCHER. Benedictine Abbey, Ottobeuren (Germany). Begun 1744. *Interior* (Schmidt-Glassner)

page 458 DOMINIKUS ZIMMERMANN. "Die Wies," Bavaria (Germany). 1745–54. *Exterior, Interior, and Plan* (Gebr. Metz; Hirmer)

459 LUIS DE ARÉVALO and F. MANUEL VASQUEZ. Cartuja, Granada (Spain). 1727–64. *Sacristy* (Mas)

460 IGNACIO VERGARA. Palace of the Marqués de Dos Aguas, Valencia (Spain). 1740–44. *Main Portal* (Marburg)

460 JAIME BORT MILIÁ. Cathedral, Murcia (Spain). 1741. *West Façade* (Kersting)

461 PETER HARRISON. Brick Market, Newport (R. I.). 1761–62. *Exterior* (Andrews)

461 Byrd House, Westover (Va.). c. 1735. *Exterior* (Andrews)

462 Keller House (Homeplace Plantation), River Road (near New Orleans, La.). *Exterior and Plan* (H.A.B.S., Johnston; H.A.B.S., Millon)

463 SAMUEL MCINTYRE. Pierce-Nichols House, Salem (Mass.). 1782. *Exterior* (Andrews)

463 THOMAS JEFFERSON. Monticello, Charlottesville (Va.). 1770–84; 1796–1808. *Garden Façade* (Andrews)

464 PIERRE CHARLES L'ENFANT. Plan for the City of Washington, D.C. 1791. (Map Division, Library of Congress)

PART FOUR

THE RENAISSANCE

18. *Early Renaissance Architecture*

ALL LOCATIONS ARE IN ITALY

FILIPPO BRUNELLESCHI. Foundling Hospital (Spedale degli Innocenti), Florence.
Designed 1419. *Exterior from northwest*

FILIPPO BRUNELLESCHI. S. Lorenzo, Florence. Designed 1418,
built 1421–60. *View of Interior toward the west*

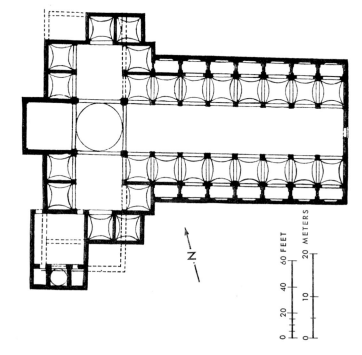

FILIPPO BRUNELLESCHI. S. Lorenzo, Florence. Designed 1418.
Plan, and Interior of Old Sacristy (1421–28) from
southwest (Sculpture by DONATELLO, *1434–43)*

FILIPPO BRUNELLESCHI. Pazzi Chapel, S. Croce, Florence. c. 1430–46; uncompleted. *View of Façade from northwest*

FILIPPO BRUNELLESCHI. Pazzi Chapel, S. Croce, Florence. c. 1430–46. *View of Interior toward northeast*

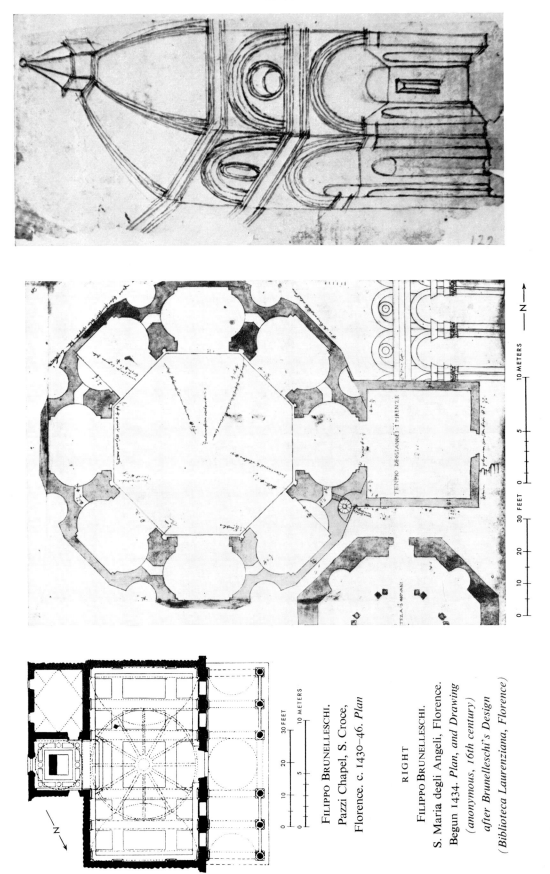

FILIPPO BRUNELLESCHI.
Pazzi Chapel, S. Croce,
Florence. c. 1430–46. *Plan*

RIGHT

FILIPPO BRUNELLESCHI.
S. Maria degli Angeli, Florence.
Begun 1434. *Plan, and Drawing
(anonymous, 16th century)
after Brunelleschi's Design
(Biblioteca Laurenziana, Florence)*

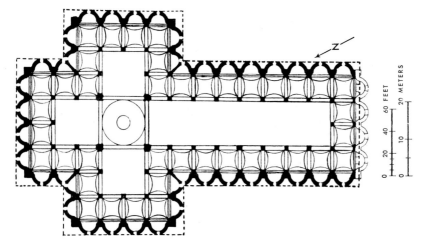

FILIPPO BRUNELLESCHI. S. Spirito,
Florence. Designed 1436;
built 1445–82. *Plan, and Interior
View toward southwest*

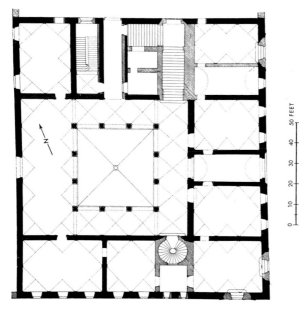

MICHELOZZO DI BARTOLOMMEO. Palazzo
Medici-Riccardi, Florence. 1444–60.
View of Exterior from the north, and Plan

MICHELOZZO
DI BARTOLOMMEO.
Palazzo Medici-Riccardi,
Florence. 1444–60.
View of Courtyard

LEONE BATTISTA ALBERTI. Palazzo Rucellai, Florence.
1446–51. *View of Façade from the south*

LEONE BATTISTA ALBERTI.
S. Francesco, Rimini.
1446–50. *View of
Exterior from southeast*

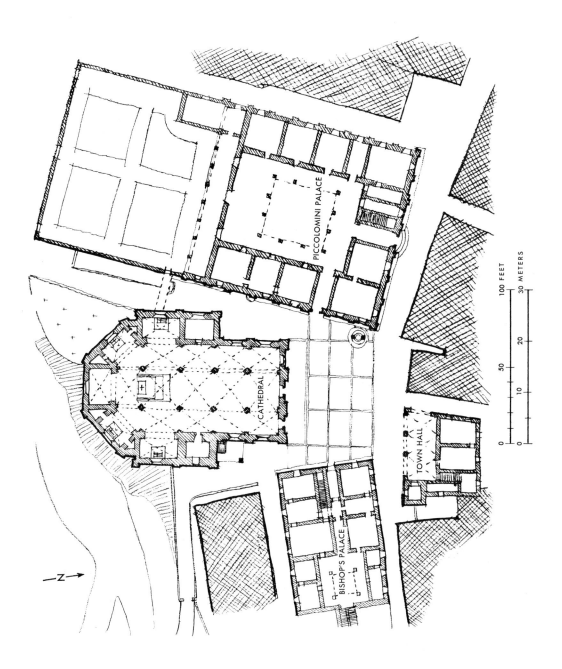

BERNARDO ROSSELLINO.
Piazza Pio II, Pienza.
1459–62. *General Plan*

Palazzo Venezia, Rome. 1465–71. *View of East Façade, and Plan*

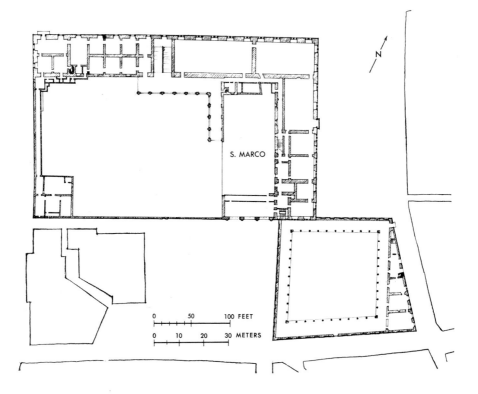

S. MARCO

0   50   100 FEET

0   10   20   30 METERS

N

ABOVE
Palazzo Venezia, Rome.
1465–71. *View of
Courtyard from southwest*

RIGHT
LEONE BATTISTA ALBERTI.
S. Andrea, Mantua.
Designed 1470; built
1472–94. *View of Façade
from southwest*

Leone Battista Alberti. S. Andrea, Mantua. Designed 1470; built 1472–94.
View of Interior toward northeast (decoration late 16th century)

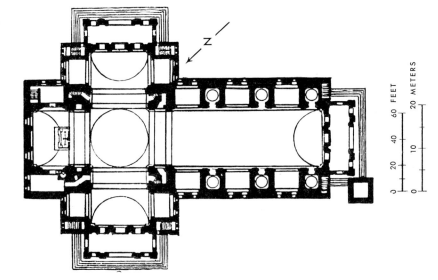

LEONE BATTISTA ALBERTI. S. Andrea, Mantua. Designed 1470; built 1472–94. *View of Interior toward the south (decoration late 16th century), and Plan*

GIULIANO DA SANGALLO. Villa Medici, Poggio a Cajano.
c. 1480. *View of Façade, and Plan*

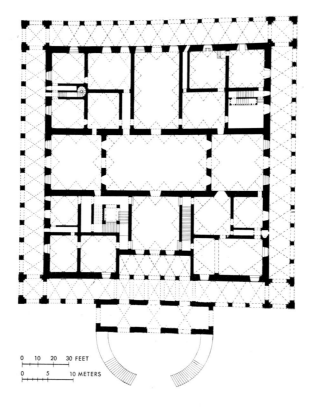

0 10 20 30 FEET

0 5 10 METERS

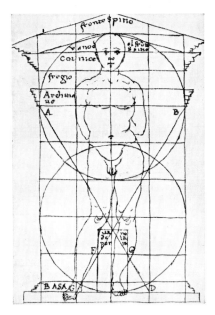
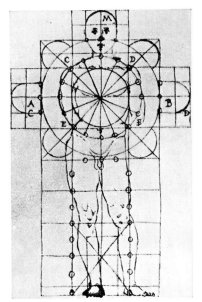

Francesco di Giorgio.
*Anthropomorphic
Derivations of Church
Façade and Church Plan.*
Pen drawings from
Trattato, fols. 39v and
43v, c. 1490–95.
*Biblioteca Nazionale,
Florence*

Giuliano da Sangallo.
S. Maria delle
Carceri, Prato.
1485–92. *View of
Exterior from
the west*

GIULIANO DA SANGALLO.
S. Maria delle Carceri,
Prato. 1485–92. *View of
Interior, and Plan* (from
Taccuino, fol. 19r).
Biblioteca Comunale, Siena

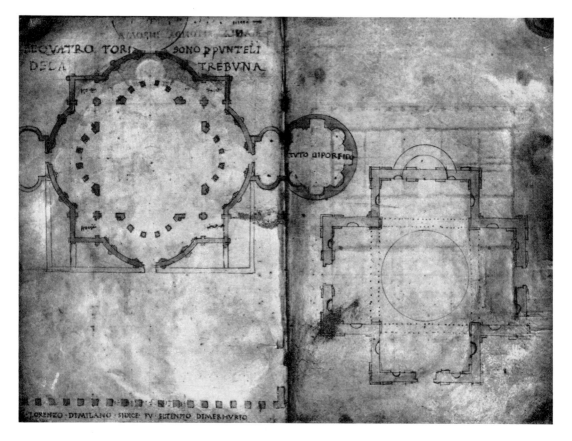

DONATO BRAMANTE. S. Maria presso
S. Satiro, Milan. c. 1480. *View of
Interior toward the east, and Plan*

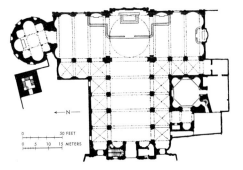

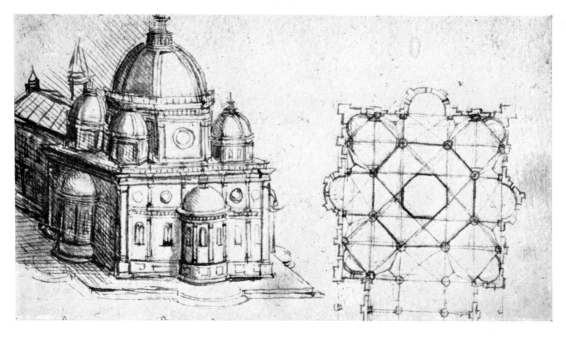

DONATO BRAMANTE. S. Maria delle Grazie,
Milan. Begun 1492. *View of Interior
toward the east, and Plan*

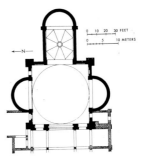

MAURO CODUCCI. S. Zaccaria, Venice. c. 1483–1500. *View of West Façade*

THE RENAISSANCE

19. *High Renaissance Architecture*

ALL LOCATIONS ARE IN ITALY

DONATO BRAMANTE. S. Maria della Pace, Rome. 1504. *View of Cloister*

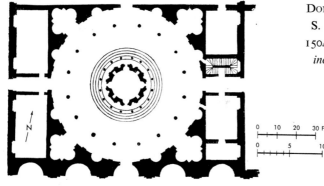

Donato Bramante. Tempietto,
S. Pietro in Montorio, Rome.
1504. *View of Exterior, and Plan
including Projected Courtyard
(after Sebastiano Serlio)*

Donato Bramante.
Belvedere Court,
Vatican City (Rome).
Begun 1503. *Portion of
North Façade, and View
in 16th Century
(anonymous drawing,
Coll. Edmonde Fatio,
Geneva)*

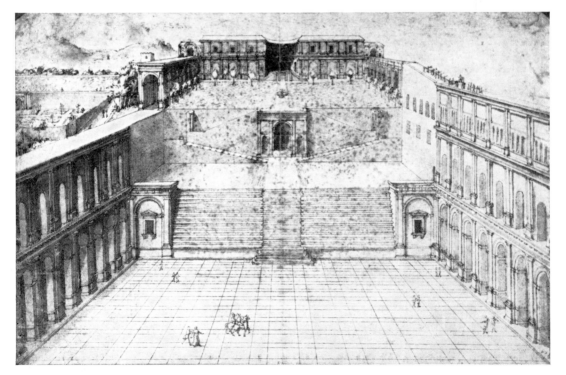

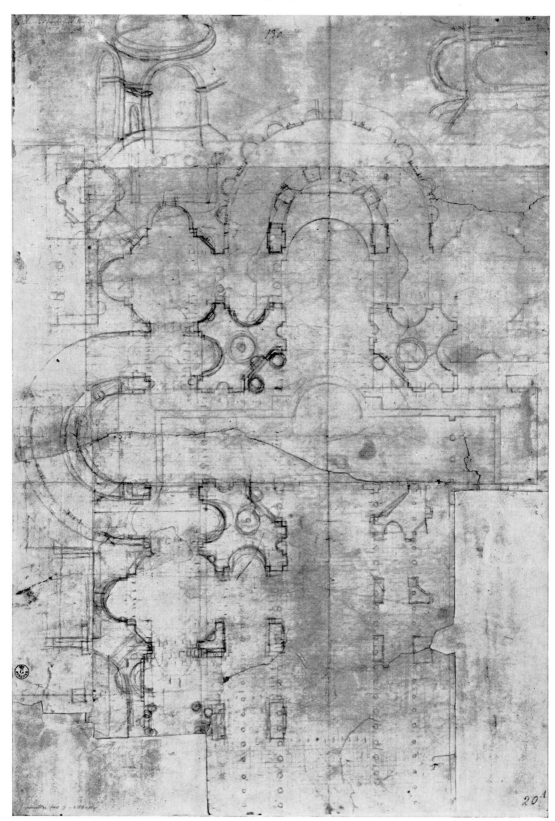

DONATO BRAMANTE. Basilica of St. Peter, Vatican City (Rome). *Plan for New Building (including foundations of Old St. Peter's)*. Pencil drawing, c. 1508. *(No. 20, Gabinetto dei Disegni, Uffizi, Florence)*

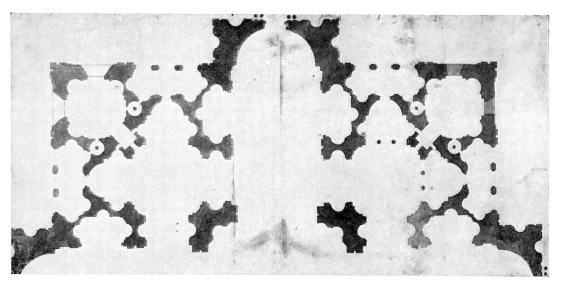

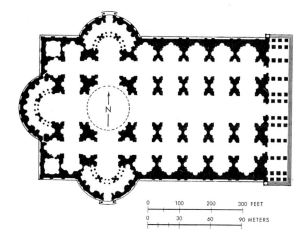

ABOVE
DONATO BRAMANTE. Basilica of
St. Peter, Vatican City (Rome).
*Original Plan, showing Alternative
Designs.* Pen and wash drawing,
1506. *(No. 1, Gabinetto dei
Disegni, Uffizi, Florence)*

CENTER LEFT
DONATO BRAMANTE. Basilica of
St. Peter. *Design for Exterior,
1506, on Bronze Medal by Caradosso
(British Museum, London)*

BELOW LEFT
RAPHAEL. Basilica of
St. Peter. *Plan, 1514–20
(after Sebastiano Serlio)*

S. Maria della Consolazione, Todi. Begun 1508. *Exterior from the east*

S. Maria della Consolazione, Todi. Begun 1508. *Interior View toward northeast*

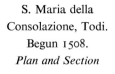

S. Maria della
Consolazione, Todi.
Begun 1508.
Plan and Section

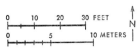

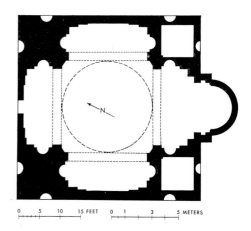

RAPHAEL. S. Eligio degli Orefici,
Rome. Begun 1509. *View into Dome,
and Plan (after Sallustio Peruzzi)*

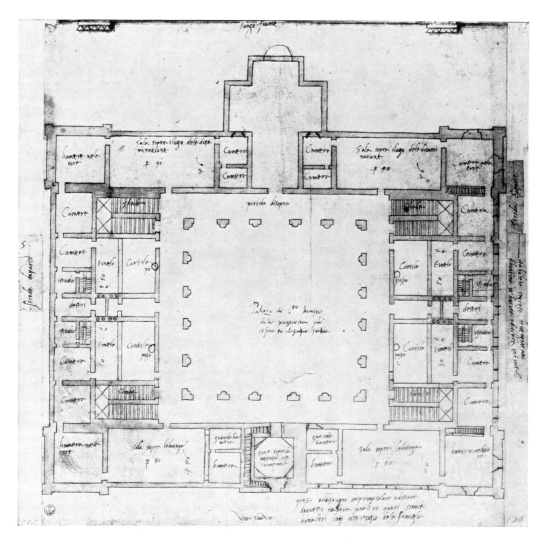

DONATO BRAMANTE. Palazzo dei Tribunali, Rome. c. 1512. *Drawing of
Plan (No. 136, Gabinetto dei Disegni, Uffizi, Florence)*

DONATO BRAMANTE. Palazzo Caprini-Raphael, Rome.
c. 1514. *Façade (engraved by Lafréry, 1549)*

RAPHAEL. Palazzo Vidoni-Caffarelli, Rome. c. 1515–20.
View of Exterior (third story added later)

THE RENAISSANCE

20. Sixteenth-Century
Architecture in Italy

ALL LOCATIONS ARE IN ITALY

ANTONIO DA SANGALLO and MICHELANGELO. Palazzo Farnese,
Rome. 1530–89. *View of Façade from the east*

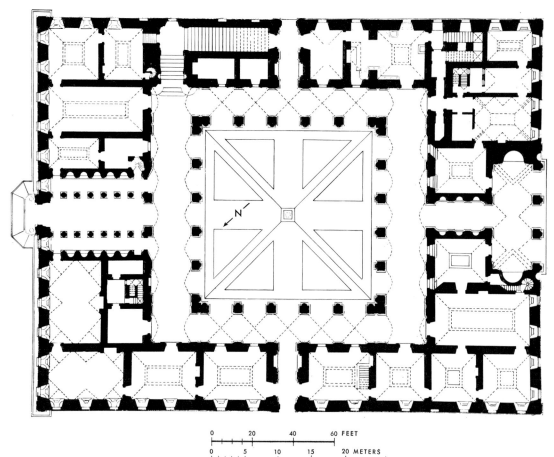

Antonio da Sangallo and Michelangelo. Palazzo Farnese,
Rome. 1530–89. *Plan, and Longitudinal Section*

ANTONIO DA SANGALLO and MICHELANGELO. Palazzo Farnese, Rome.
1530–89. *View of Courtyard*

ANTONIO DA SANGALLO.
Piazza Farnese, Rome.
1535–50. *General Plan*

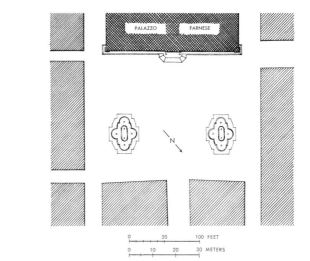

MICHELANGELO. Laurentian Library, Florence. 1524.
Interior View of Entry Hall and Staircase

GIULIO ROMANO. Palazzo del Tè, Mantua. 1525–35.
Portion of East Wall of Courtyard

JACOPO SANSOVINO. Library of St. Mark, Venice.
Begun 1536. *Exterior from the south*

BALDASSARE PERUZZI. Palazzo Massimi, Rome. Begun 1535. *View of Façade from southwest*

MICHELANGELO. Palazzo dei Conservatori, The Capitol, Rome. 1538–61.
View of Exterior from northeast

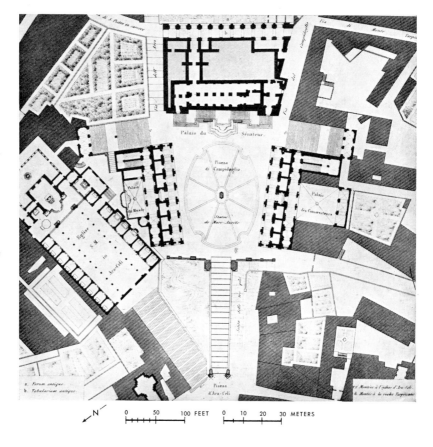

MICHELANGELO.
The Capitol, Rome.
Designed 1537. *Bird's-
Eye View (engraved
by Etienne Dupérac,
1569), and
General Plan*

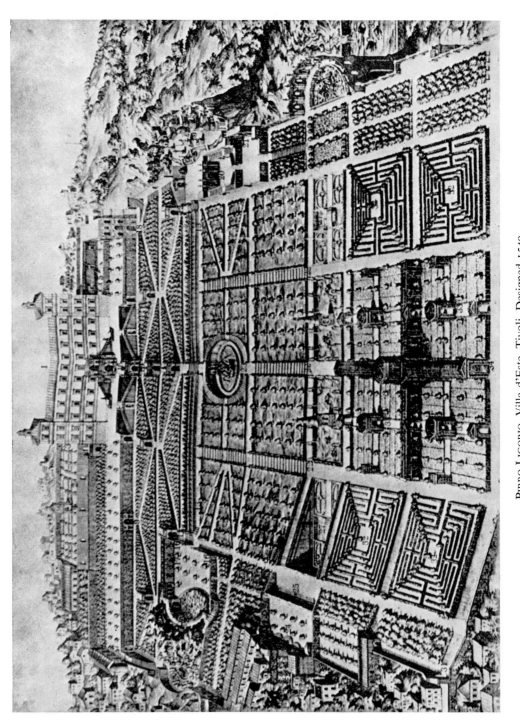

PIRRO LIGORIO. Villa d'Este, Tivoli. Designed 1549.
Bird's-Eye View from northwest (engraved by Etienne Dupérac)

GIORGIO VASARI, GIACOMO VIGNOLA, and BARTOLOMMEO AMMANATI.
Villa Giulia, Rome. 1550–55. *View of Garden Façade from
southeast, Longitudinal Section, and Plan*

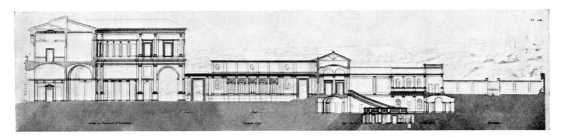

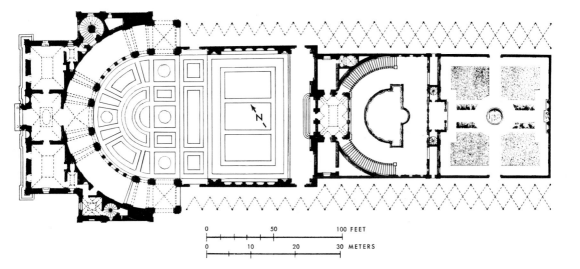

GIORGIO VASARI. Uffizi Palace, Florence. Begun 1560. *Exterior from northeast, and View through Loggia toward the Arno River*

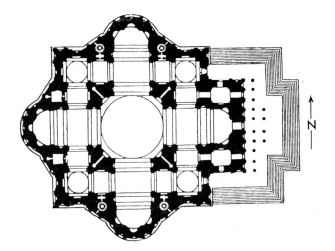

MICHELANGELO. Basilica of
St. Peter, Vatican City (Rome).
1546–64; completed 1590
by GIACOMO DELLA PORTA.
*Exterior and Dome from
southwest, and Plan
(after Dupérac and Lafréry, 1569)*

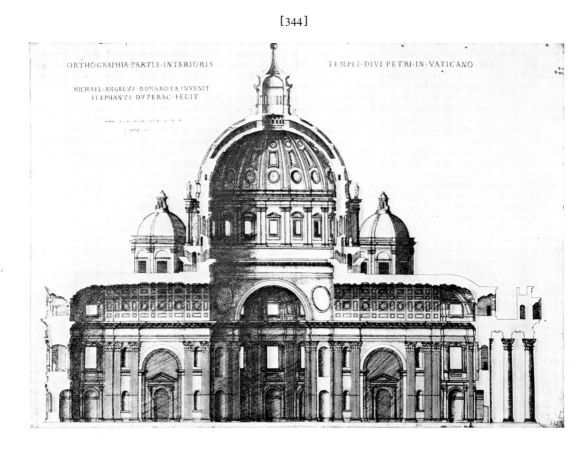

ORTHOGRAPHIA·PARTIS·INTERIORIS   TEMPLI·DIVI·PETRI·IN·VATICANO

MICHAEL·ANGELVS·BONAROTA·INVENIT
STEPHANVS·DVPERAC·FECIT

MICHELANGELO. Basilica of
St. Peter, Vatican
City (Rome). 1546–64.
*Longitudinal Section
(engraved by Etienne
Dupérac, 1569), and
Interior View of
Crossing from northwest*

GUIDO GUIDETTI. S. Caterina dei Funari, Rome.
Begun 1564. *View of Façade from the south*

ANDREA PALLADIO.
Villa Rotonda, Vicenza.
Begun 1550. *View of
Exterior from southeast,
Plan, and Section*

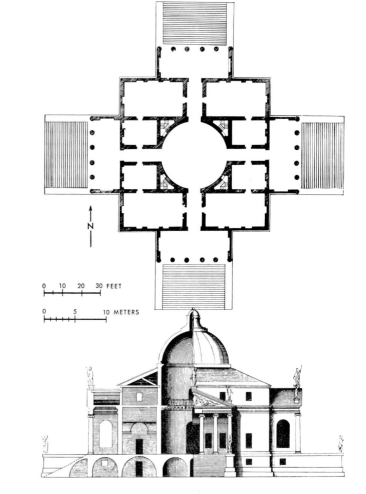

Andrea Palladio. S. Giorgio Maggiore, Venice.
Designed 1565. *View of Façade from the northwest*

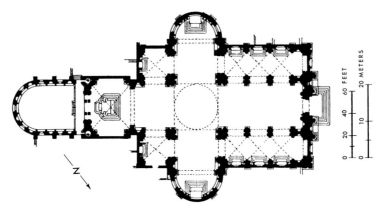

Andrea Palladio. S. Giorgio Maggiore, Venice. Designed 1565.
View of Interior toward southeast (apse), and Plan

ANDREA PALLADIO. Teatro Olimpico, Vicenza. 1580–84. *View of Stage*

GIACOMO VIGNOLA and
GIACOMO DELLA PORTA.
Church of the Gesù, Rome.
c. 1575–84. *View of Interior
toward the east (above),
Plan (by Vignola),
and View of Façade
(by della Porta)*

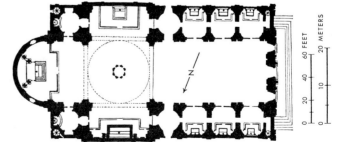

ANDREA SACCHI and JAN MIEL. *Pope Urban VIII Visiting Il Gesù.*
Oil painting, 1639–41. *National Gallery, Rome*

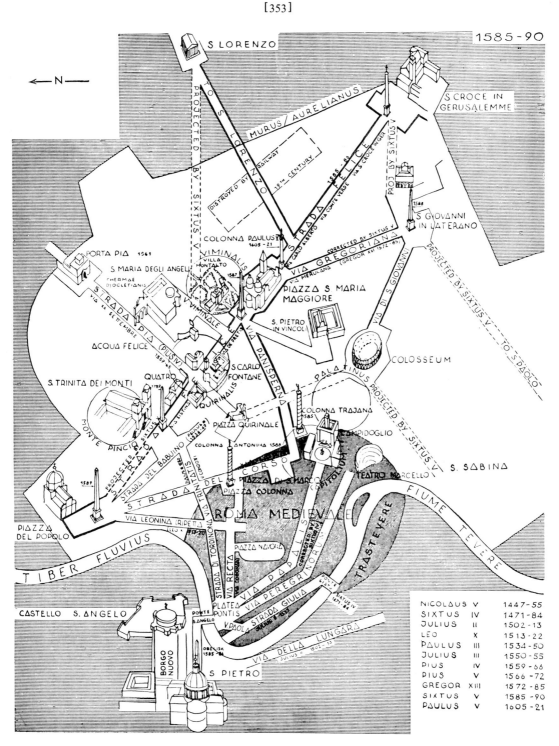

DOMENICO FONTANA and POPE SIXTUS V. *Plan for New Avenues in Rome.* 1585–90.

Vincenzo Scamozzi. City of Palmanova (Veneto). 1593. *Air View*

THE RENAISSANCE

21. Sixteenth-Century Architecture outside Italy

Château of Blois (France). Wing of Francis I, 1515–24.
Spiral Staircase Tower in Courtyard, from southeast

DOMENICO DA CORTONA (?). Château of Chambord (France).
Begun 1519. *View of Exterior from the north*

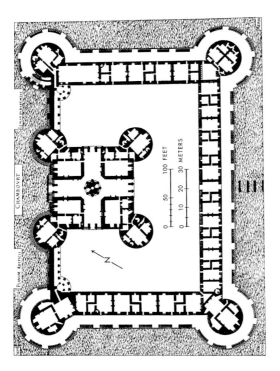

Domenico da Cortona (?). Château of
Chambord (France). Begun 1519.
Plan, and Central Double Staircase

GILLES LE BRETON. Château of
Fontainebleau (France). Begun 1528.
*Stairs, by Jean Ducerceau,
in Cour du Cheval Blanc*

BELOW
GILLES LE BRETON and
PHILIBERT DE L'ORME. Château of
Fontainebleau (France). 1540–56. *View
of Ballroom (Galerie de Henri II);
Decorations by* PRIMATICCIO *(1552–56)*

HECTOR SOHIER. St. Pierre, Caen (France). 1528–45.
Exterior View of Apse and Chapels

PHILIBERT DE L'ORME. Château of Anet (France).
Main Gate, 1552. *Exterior View (tympanum
sculpture by* BENVENUTO CELLINI)

PHILIBERT DE L'ORME. Château of Anet (France). Frontispiece,
completed before 1550. *View, as reerected in courtyard of
École des Beaux-Arts, Paris (sculptural decoration by* JEAN GOUJON)

PIERRE LESCOT. The Louvre, Paris (France). *Southwest Façade of Square Court (begun 1546), and Air View from the west*

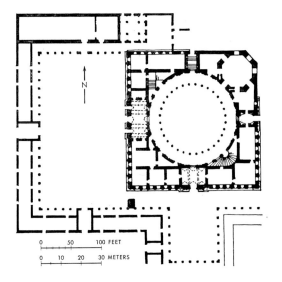

PEDRO MACHUCA. Palace of Charles V,
Granada (Spain). Begun 1527.
View of Circular Courtyard, and Plan

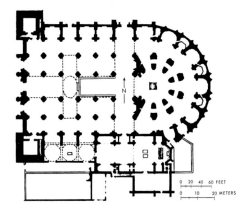

DIEGO DA SILOE.
Cathedral, Granada
(Spain). Begun 1529.
*View of Interior
toward the northwest,
and Plan*

JUAN DE HERRERA and JUAN BAUTISTA DE TOLEDO. Escorial (near Madrid, Spain).
1563–82. *General View of Exterior from the north, and Plan*

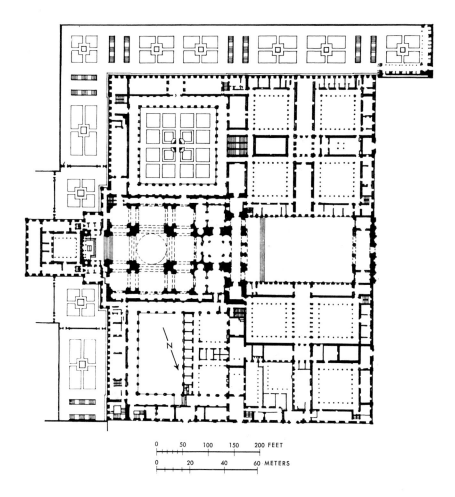

Diogo de Torralva. Cristo Monastery, Tomar (Portugal). 1557–62. *View of Main Courtyard from above*

Juan de Herrera and Juan Bautista de Toledo. Church, Escorial (near Madrid, Spain). 1572–85. *View of Interior at Crossing*

Francisco Becerra. Cathedral, Cuzco (Peru). 1582–1654. *View of Interior*

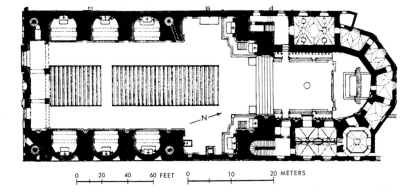

Wolfgang Miller and
Friedrich Sustris.
St. Michael, Munich.
1582–97. *View of
Interior, and Plan*

0   20   40   60 FEET   0   10   20 METERS

ELIAS HOLL. Town Hall, Augsburg (Germany). 1610–20.
View of Rear Façade

Elias Holl. Town Hall, Augsburg (Germany). 1615–20. *Interior View of Golden Hall*

Wollaton Hall, Nottinghamshire (England). 1580–88. *Exterior View from the east*

Burghley House, Northamptonshire (England). 1585. *View of*
Courtyard toward the east, including Central Pavilion

THE RENAISSANCE

22. *Architecture of the Seventeenth Century in Italy*

ALL LOCATIONS ARE IN ITALY

CARLO MADERNO. S. Susanna, Rome. 1597–1603.
View of Façade from southeast

CARLO MADERNO.
Basilica of
St. Peter, Vatican
City (Rome). 1606–12.
*View of Main Façade
from the east*

CARLO MADERNO.
Basilica of
St. Peter, Vatican
City (Rome). 1606–12.
View of Interior
toward the west

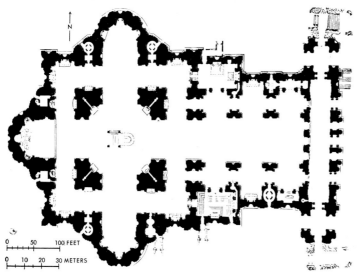

ABOVE
Basilica of St. Peter,
Vatican City (Rome).
*View of Interior toward the
west, showing Tabernacle
by* GIANLORENZO BERNINI
(begun 1624)

LEFT
Basilica of St. Peter.
*Plan, showing Additions
by* CARLO MADERNO
(1606–12)

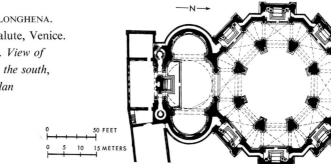

BALDASSARE LONGHENA.
S. Maria della Salute, Venice.
Begun 1631. *View of
Exterior from the south,
and Plan*

—N→

0   50 FEET

0   5   10   15 METERS

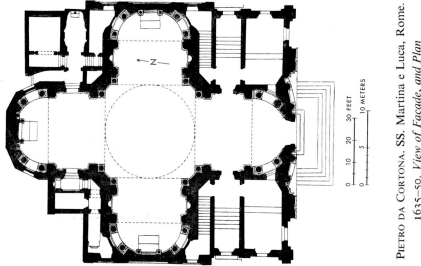

PIETRO DA CORTONA. SS. Martina e Luca, Rome.
1635–50. *View of Façade, and Plan*

BELOW
PIETRO DA CORTONA. SS. Martina e Luca, Rome.
1635–50. *View of Interior toward the Apse*

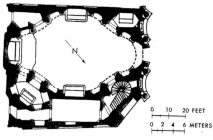

FRANCESCO BORROMINI. S. Carlo alle
Quattro Fontane, Rome. Begun 1635.
View into Dome, and Plan

FRANCESCO BORROMINI. S. Carlo alle Quattro Fontane, Rome.

View of Façade from the north (1667)

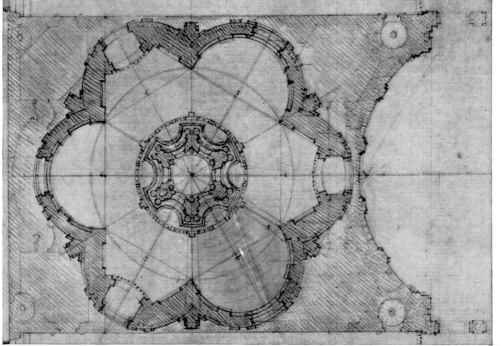

FRANCESCO BORROMINI. S. Ivo della Sapienza, Rome. 1642–50. Plan
Drawing by Borromini (Albertina, Vienna), and Transverse Section

FRANCESCO BORROMINI. S. Ivo della Sapienza, Rome. 1642–50.
View from Courtyard toward the east

FRANCESCO BORROMINI and CARLO RAINALDI. S. Agnese in Piazza Navona, Rome. Begun 1652. *View of Façade from southeast, and Plan*

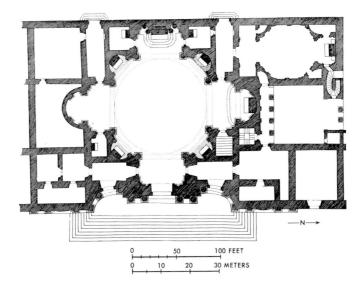

PIETRO DA CORTONA.
S. Maria della Pace, Rome.
1656–57. *View of Façade
from southeast, and Plan*

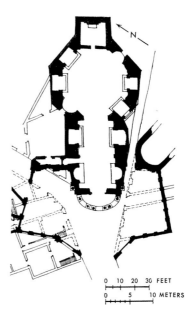

Basilica of St. Peter,
Vatican City (Rome).
*Air View: Nave and
Façade by* CARLO MADERNO,
*1606–12; Piazza
San Pietro by* BERNINI,
designed 1657

GIANLORENZO BERNINI.
Basilica of St. Peter.
*Colonnades of Piazza
San Pietro, designed 1657*

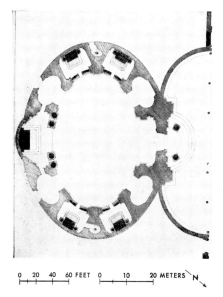

0 20 40 60 FEET 0   10   20 METERS N

GIANLORENZO BERNINI.
S. Andrea al Quirinale,
Rome. 1658–70. *View of
Façade from the north
and Interior toward
southeast, and Plan*

GIANLORENZO BERNINI. Palazzo Chigi-Odescalchi, Rome. Begun 1664. *View of Exterior*

GUARINO GUARINI. S. Lorenzo,
Turin. 1666–79. *View into Dome,
and Plan*

GUARINO GUARINI.
Chapel of the Holy Shroud
(Cappella della
Santissima Sindone),
Cathedral, Turin.
1667–94. *Exterior View,
and View into Dome*

GUARINO GUARINI.
Palazzo Carignano, Turin.
1679–92. *View of Exterior
from the north, and Plan*

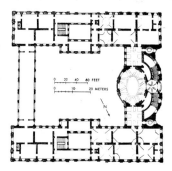

GUARINO GUARINI. Palazzo Carignano, Turin. 1679–92. *View of Main Staircase*

THE RENAISSANCE

23. *Seventeenth-Century*
Architecture in
France and England

Place des Vosges, Paris (France). Begun 1605. *Air View from southeast*

SALOMON DE BROSSE (?). St. Gervais, Paris (France). 1616.
View of West Façade (addition to Late Gothic church)

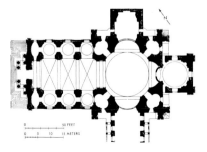

FRANÇOIS MANSART and JACQUES LEMERCIER.
Church of the Val-de-Grâce, Paris
(France). 1645–62. *View of Exterior,
and Plan (engraved by Jean Marot)*

FRANÇOIS MANSART and JACQUES LEMERCIER. Church of the Val-de-Grâce,
Paris (France). 1645–62. *View of Interior toward the Apse*

FRANÇOIS MANSART. Château of Maisons (near Paris, France).
1642–46. *Main Entrance Court from southeast, and Interior of
Vestibule toward southwest*

Louis Le Vau. Château of Vaux-le-Vicomte (near Melun,
France). 1657–61. *View of Exterior, and Plan*

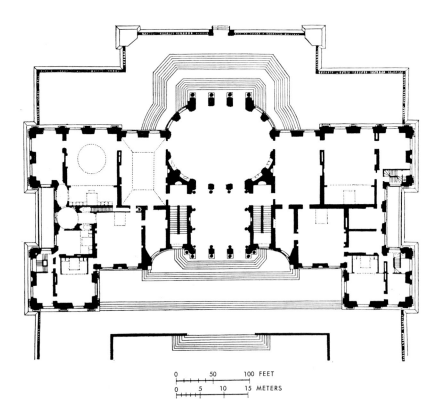

0   50   100 FEET
0   5   10   15 METERS

GIANLORENZO BERNINI. East Façade of the Louvre, Paris (France).
Drawing for Second Project, 1665 (Royal Museum, Stockholm)

LOUIS LE VAU. Château of Versailles (France). Begun 1669.
Garden Façade (engraved by Israel Silvestre)

LOUIS LE VAU and JULES HARDOUIN-MANSART. Château of Versailles (France).
1669–85. *View of Garden Façade from the west*

Louis Le Vau and Jules Hardouin-Mansart. Château of Versailles (France).
1669–85. *Air View from the west, and Interior View of Hall of Mirrors*
(Galerie des Glaces; begun 1678)

JULES HARDOUIN-MANSART, CHARLES LEBRUN, and ANTOINE COYSEVOX.
Salon de la Guerre, Château of Versailles (France). Begun 1678.
View of Interior toward the north

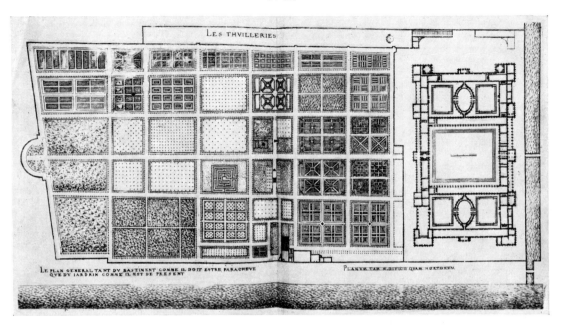

Tuileries Gardens, Paris (France). Mid-16th century.
Plan (engraved by Ducerceau)

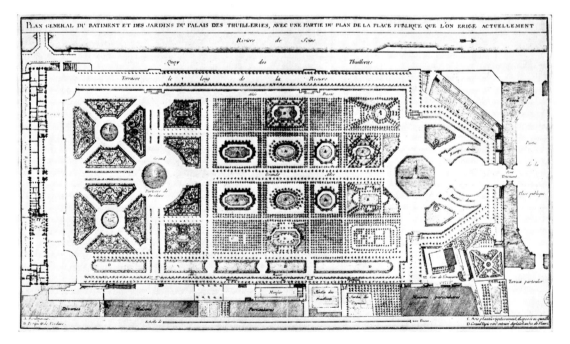

ANDRÉ LE NÔTRE. Tuileries Gardens, Paris (France). 1664–72.
Plan (engraved by Blondel)

ANDRÉ LE NÔTRE. Gardens, Château of Versailles (France).
Begun 1667. *Plan (engraved 1693)*

CLAUDE PERRAULT. East Façade of the Louvre, Paris (France). 1667–70.

JULES HARDOUIN-MANSART. Church of the Invalides
(St. Louis des Invalides), Paris (France). 1680–91.
Plan, Longitudinal Section, and View of Exterior from the north

JULES HARDOUIN-MANSART. Place Vendôme, Paris (France). 1698. *Air View from southwest*

INIGO JONES. Banqueting House, Whitehall Palace,
London (England). 1619–22. *West Façade*

ABOVE

SIR CHRISTOPHER WREN.
Hampton Court Palace
(England). Designed
1689. *View of
Exterior from southeast*

LEFT

SIR CHRISTOPHER WREN.
Cathedral of St. Paul,
London (England).
1675–1710. *West Façade*

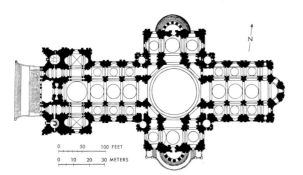

Sir Christopher Wren.
Cathedral of St. Paul,
London (England). 1675–1710.
*View of Interior toward
the east, and Plan*

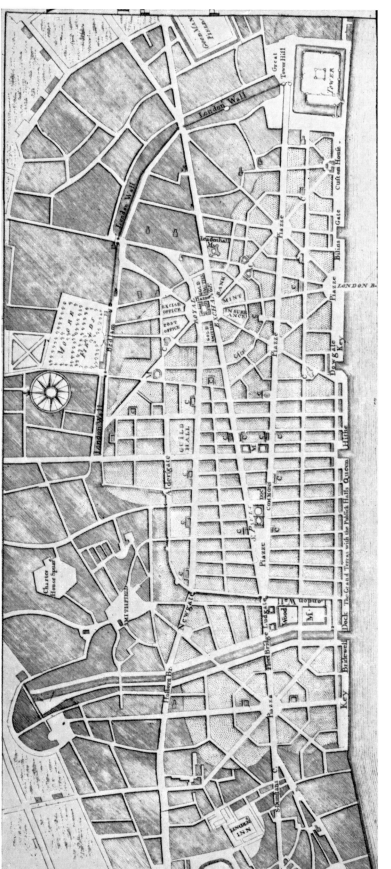

SIR CHRISTOPHER WREN. *Plan for the Rebuilding of London after the Great Fire of 1666 (engraved 1758)*

THE RENAISSANCE

24. Seventeenth-Century Architecture in Flanders, Holland, Spain, Germany, Austria, and the New World

FRANCESCO CARATTI. Czernin Palace, Prague (Czechoslovakia).
Begun 1667. *View of Façade*

ANDREAS SCHLUETER. Royal Palace, Berlin (Germany). 1698–1706. *South Façade*

JOHANN LUKAS VON HILDEBRANDT. St. Lawrence, Gabel (Czechoslovakia).
Begun 1699. *View of Exterior*

RIGHT
JOHANN LUKAS VON HILDEBRANDT. St. Lawrence, Gabel (Czechoslovakia).
Begun 1699. *View of Interior, Plan, and Longitudinal Section*

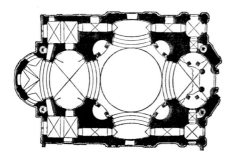

Johann Fischer
von Erlach.
Schloss Frain (Moravia,
Czechoslovakia).
1689–95. *View of
Exterior from the east,
and Interior of
Grand Salon*

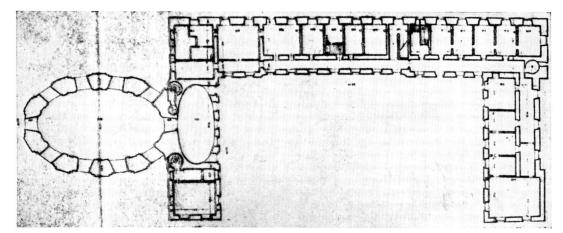

JOHANN FISCHER VON ERLACH. Schloss Frain
(Moravia, Czechoslovakia). 1689–95. *Plan*

JOHANN FISCHER VON ERLACH. Church of the Holy Trinity,
Salzburg (Austria). 1694–1702. *View of Façade*

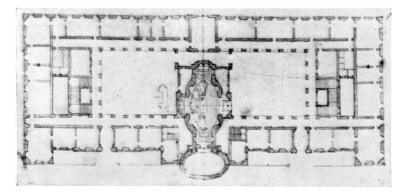

JOHANN FISCHER
VON ERLACH.
Church of the
Holy Trinity, Salzburg
(Austria). 1694–1702.
*View of Interior of
Church, and Drawing of
Building Complex*

WILLIAM HESIUS. St. Michel, Louvain (Belgium). 1650. *View of Façade*

JACOB VAN CAMPEN and PIETER POST. Mauritshuis, The Hague (Holland).
1633. *View of Canal Façade*

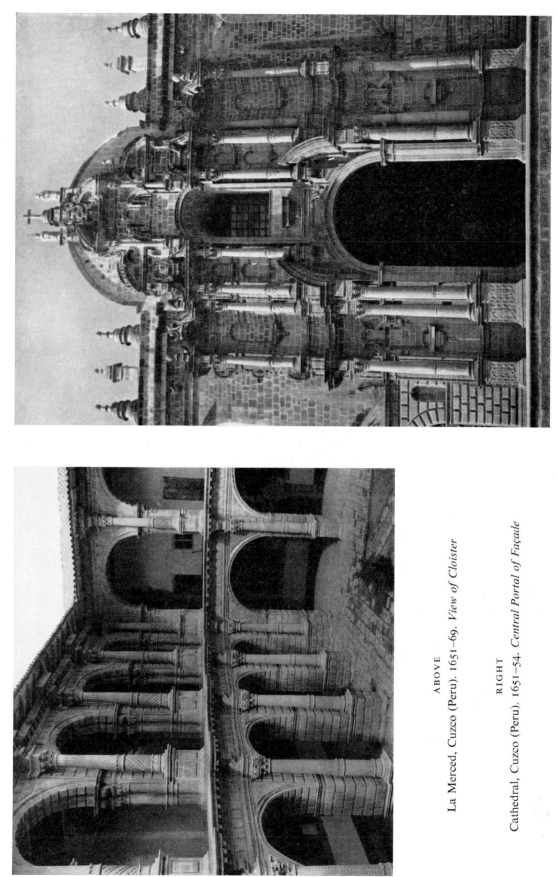

ABOVE

La Merced, Cuzco (Peru). 1651–69. *View of Cloister*

RIGHT

Cathedral, Cuzco (Peru). 1651–54. *Central Portal of Façade*

THE RENAISSANCE

25. Eighteenth-Century Architecture in Europe and the New World

Nicola Salvi. Trevi Fountain, Rome (Italy). 1732–36. *View from southeast*

ALESSANDRO SPECCHI. Porta di Ripetta, Rome (Italy). Built 1703;
now destroyed. *Vieuw (engraved by Alessandro Specchi)*

FILIPPO JUVARRA. Superga, Turin (Italy). 1717–31. *Exterior View from southwest*

FILIPPO JUVARRA. Royal Hunting Palace, Stupinigi (near Turin, Italy).
1729–33. *Interior of Great Hall*

FILIPPO JUVARRA. Royal Hunting Palace, Stupinigi (near Turin, Italy).
1729–33. *Air View, and View of Exterior*

FILIPPO JUVARRA. Church of the Carmine, Turin (Italy).
1732–35. *View of Interior toward the east*

ALESSANDRO GALILEI. S. Giovanni in Laterano, Rome
(Italy). 1733–36. *Central Portion of East Façade*

FERDINANDO FUGA. S. Maria Maggiore, Rome (Italy).
1741–43. *View of Façade from southeast*

PIETRO PASSALACQUA and DOMENICO GREGORINI. S. Croce in Gerusalemme,
Rome (Italy). 1743. *View of Façade from the west*

FRANCESCO DE SANCTIS. Spanish Steps, Rome (Italy). 1723–25.
General View toward the east

FILIPPO RAGUZZINI. Piazza S. Ignazio, Rome (Italy). 1727–28.
View toward the north, and Plan

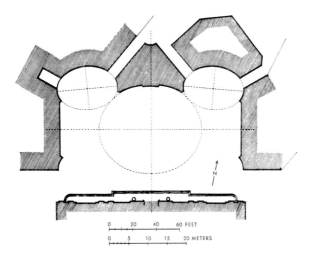

FERDINANDO FUGA. Palazzo della Consulta, Rome (Italy). 1732–37.
View of Façade from northwest

GABRIELI VALVASSORI. Palazzo Doria-Pamphili,
Rome (Italy). 1731–34. *View of Portion of Façade*

GABRIELI VALVASSORI. Palazzo Doria-Pamphili,
Rome (Italy). 1731–34. *Interior of Main Gallery*

LUIGI VANVITELLI. Royal Palace, Caserta (Italy).
1752–74. *View of Main Staircase*

GIOVANNI BATTISTA PIRANESI. S. Maria del Priorato, Rome (Italy).
1765 (renovation of earlier church). *View of Façade from southwest*

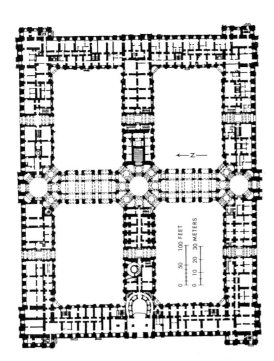

Luigi Vanvitelli. Royal Palace, Caserta (Italy).
1752–74. *View of Main Façade from the south, and Plan*

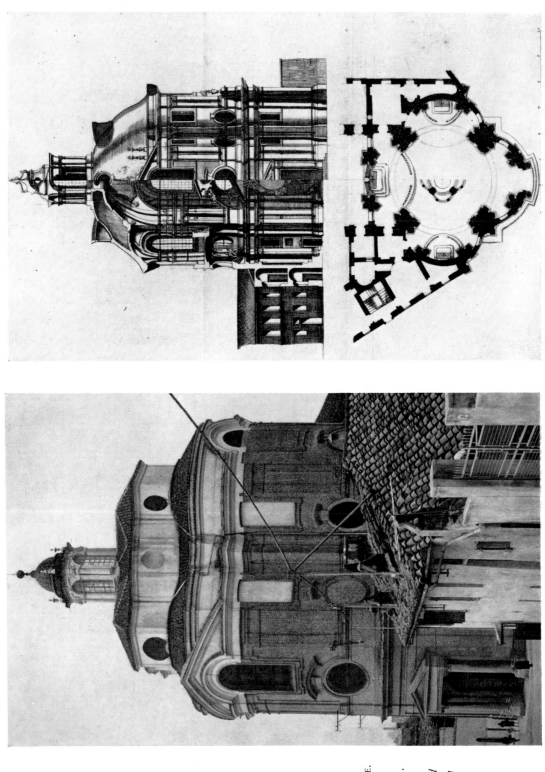

BERNARDO VITTONE.
S. Chiara, Brà
(Italy). Begun 1742.
View of Exterior,
Engraved Plan, and
Transverse Section

BERNARDO VITTONE. S. Chiara, Brà (Italy). Begun 1742. *View of Upper Interior*

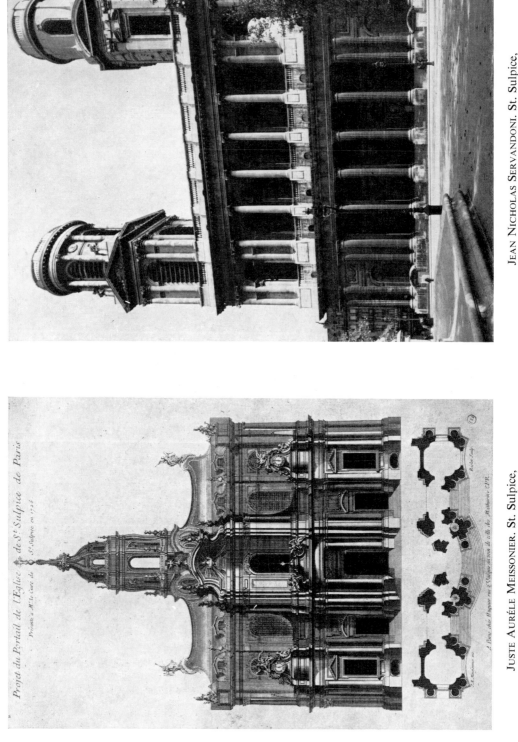

JEAN NICHOLAS SERVANDONI. St. Sulpice,
Paris (France). 1733. *View of Façade*

JUSTE AURÉLE MEISSONIER. St. Sulpice,
Paris (France). *Design for Façade, 1726*

GERMAIN BOFFRAND.
Hôtel de Soubise,
Paris (France).
Begun 1732. *Interior of
Salon de la Princesse*

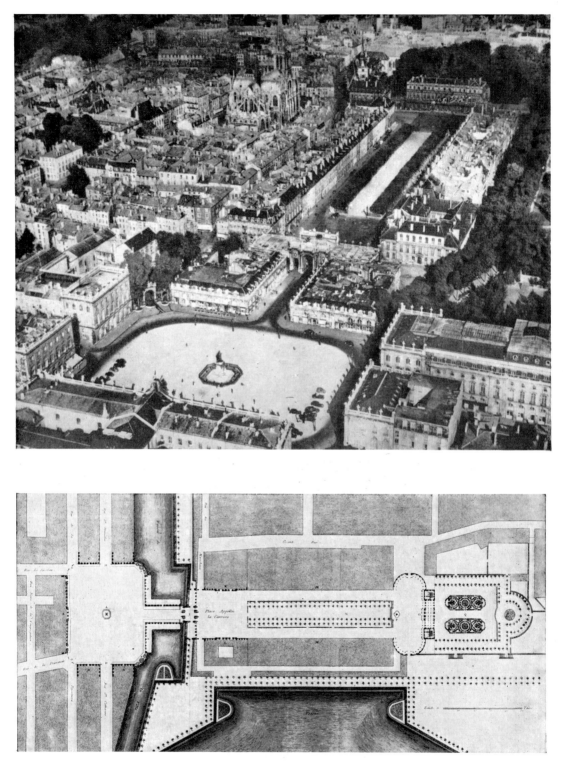

EMMANUEL HÉRÉ DE CORNY. Place de la Carrière and Hemicycle, Nancy (France).
1751–59. *Air View from the east, and Engraved Plan*

Jacques Ange Gabriel.
Petit Trianon,
Versailles (France).
1762–64. *View of
Garden Façade, and Plan*

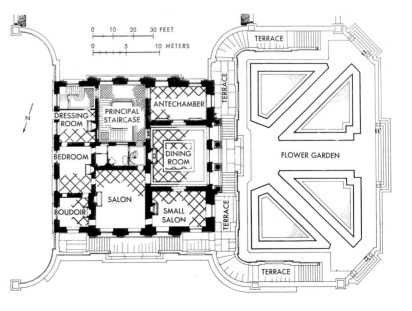

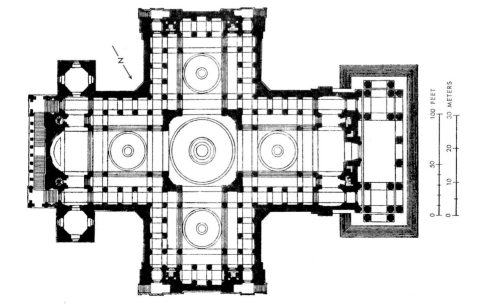

JACQUES GERMAIN SOUFFLOT. The Panthéon
(Ste. Geneviève), Paris (France). 1755–92.
Plan, and View of Interior toward the east

RICHARD MIQUE. Le Hameau, Versailles (France). 1783. *General View of Exterior*

RIGHT
JAMES GIBBS.
St. Martin-in-the-Fields,
London (England). 1721–26.
View of Façade

BELOW
JOHN WOOD THE ELDER and
JOHN WOOD THE YOUNGER.
The Circus and the Royal
Crescent, Bath (England).
c. 1754–75. *Air View*

ABOVE
ROBERT ADAM. Home House,
London (England). 1772–73.
Interior of Front Drawing Room

RIGHT
ROBERT ADAM.
House in the Adelphi,
London (England). 1768–72.
View of Façade

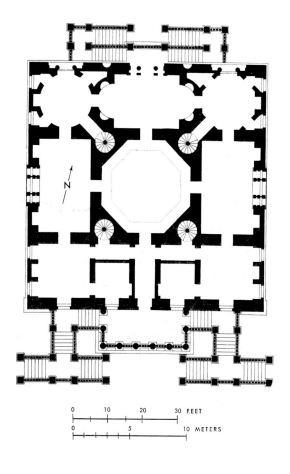

RICHARD BOYLE, EARL OF BURLINGTON,
and WILLIAM KENT. Chiswick House,
Chiswick (near London, England).
Begun 1725. *View of Façade,
and Engraved Plan*

| 0 | 10 | 20 | 30 FEET |
| 0 | | 5 | 10 METERS |

SIR JOHN VANBRUGH. Blenheim Palace, Woodstock (Oxfordshire, England).
Begun 1705. *Garden Façade from southeast, and Entrance Façade
in Great Court from northeast*

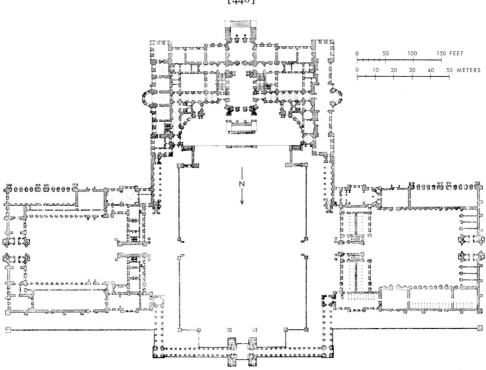

SIR JOHN VANBRUGH. Blenheim Palace, Woodstock (Oxfordshire, England).
Begun 1705. *Engraved Plan showing Original Design*

JAKOB PRANDTAUER. Benedictine Abbey, Melk (Austria). Begun 1702.
View from the Danube River, toward southeast

LEFT
Strawberry Hill, Twickenham (England). Enlarged and "gothicized"
1750–70, by HORACE WALPOLE. *Interior of Holbein Chamber*

JAKOB PRANDTAUER.
Benedictine Abbey, Melk (Austria).
1702–c. 1738. *Plans of Building Complex
and of Monastery Church, and Interior of
Church toward southeast (decorations
by* BEDUZZI *and* MUNGGENAST*)*

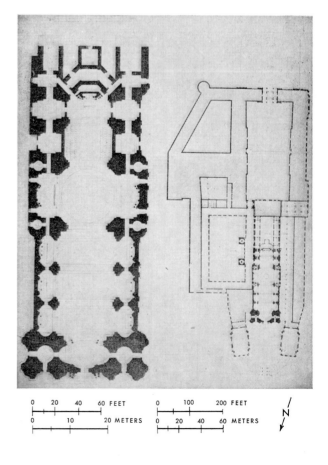

0	20	40	60 FEET
0		10	20 METERS

0		100		200 FEET
0	20	40	60 METERS	

N

JOHANN FISCHER VON ERLACH.
St. Charles Borromaeus,
Vienna (Austria). 1716–37.
*View of Façade from northwest,
and Plan*

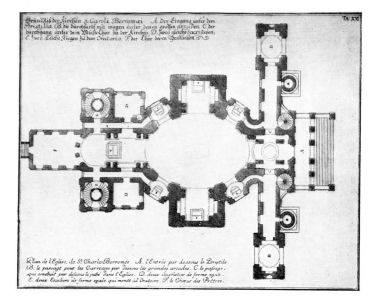

JOHANN FISCHER VON ERLACH. St. Charles Borromaeus,
Vienna (Austria). 1716–37. *View of Interior toward southeast*

JOHANN LUKAS VON HILDEBRANDT. Upper Palace, Belvedere, Vienna (Austria). 1721–24. *View of Garden Façade, and Interior of Garden Room (entrance hall)*

MATTHÄUS DANIEL PÖPPELMANN. The Zwinger, Dresden (Germany).
1711–22. *Exterior View of a Pavilion*

COSMAS DAMIAN ASAM and EGID QUIRIN ASAM. Abbey Church,
Rohr (Bavaria, Germany). 1717–21. *View of High Altar,*
with The Assumption *(sculptured group)*

BALTHASAR NEUMANN. Episcopal Palace, Würzburg (Germany). 1719–44.
Interior of Kaisersaal (frescoes by G. B. TIEPOLO, *1751)*

BALTHASAR NEUMANN. Episcopal Palace, Würzburg (Germany). 1719–44.
View of Central Staircase

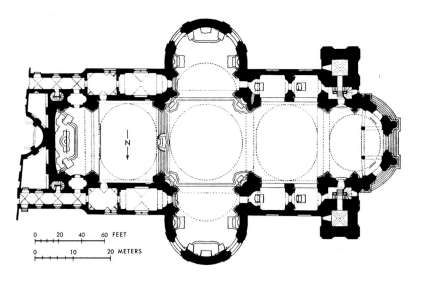

JOHANN MICHAEL FISCHER. Benedictine Abbey, Ottobeuren (Germany).
Begun 1744. *Interior View of Church toward the east* (above),
Exterior of Abbey Church from northwest, and Plan (left)

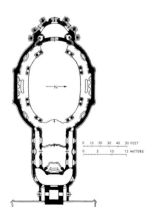

Luis de Arévalo and F. Manuel Vasquez. Cartuja (Charterhouse),
Granada (Spain). 1727–64. *View of Interior of Sacristy*

LEFT
Dominikus Zimmermann. "Die Wies" (Pilgrimage Church on River Wies), Bavaria
(Germany). 1745–54. *Exterior from southwest, Interior toward the east, and Plan*

JAIME BORT MILIÁ. Cathedral, Murcia (Spain).
1741. *View of West Façade*

IGNACIO VERGARA. Palace of the Marqués de Dos Aguas,
Valencia (Spain). 1740–44. *Main Portal*
(designed by H. R. Brocandel)

Byrd House, Westover (Charles City County, Va.).
c. 1735. *View of Exterior from the north*

Peter Harrison. Brick Market, Newport (R.I.).
1761–62. *View of Exterior*

Keller House (Homeplace Plantation), River Road (near New Orleans, La.).
View of Exterior from the east, and Plan

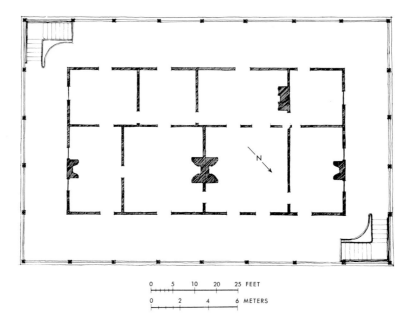

SAMUEL McINTYRE. Pierce-Nichols House, Salem (Mass.). 1782. *View of Exterior*

THOMAS JEFFERSON. Monticello, Charlottesville (Va.). 1770–84;
1796–1808. *View of Garden Façade from northwest*

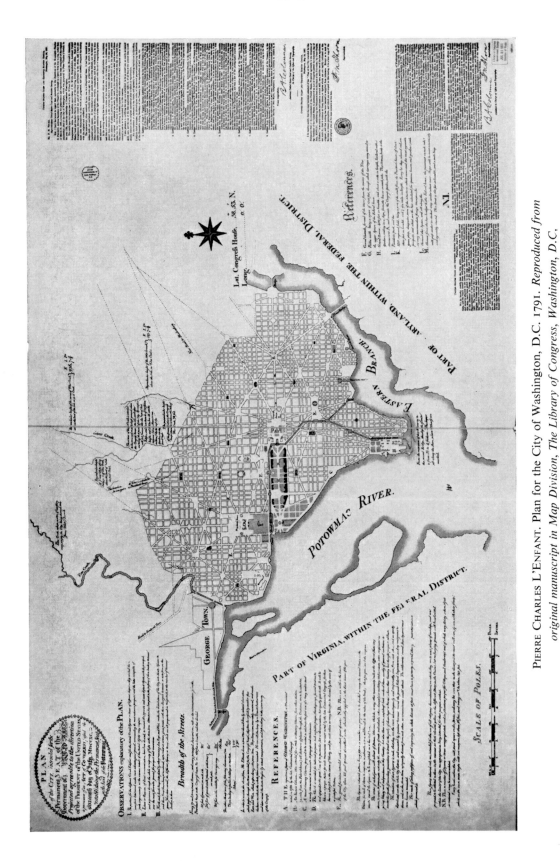

PIERRE CHARLES L'ENFANT. Plan for the City of Washington, D.C. 1791. *Reproduced from original manuscript in Map Division, The Library of Congress, Washington, D.C.*

PART FIVE

THE MODERN WORLD

LIST OF ILLUSTRATIONS

26. NINETEENTH-CENTURY ARCHITECTURE IN ENGLAND, FRANCE, AND THE UNITED STATES OF AMERICA

page 469 CHARLES PERCIER and PIERRE F. L. FONTAINE. Rue de Rivoli, Paris (France). 1802–55. *View* (Roubier)

470 JOHN NASH. Regent Street, London (England). 1811–35. *Plan* (Summerson, *Georgian London*, fig. 25)

471 JOHN NASH. The Royal Pavilion, Brighton (England). 1815–18. *East Façade* (Edwin Smith)

471 SIR ROBERT SMIRKE. British Museum, London (England). Begun 1824. *South Façade* (Edwin Smith)

472 BENJAMIN LATROBE. Catholic Cathedral, Baltimore (Md.). Begun 1805. *Exterior and Interior* (Schaefer)

473 WILLIAM STRICKLAND. Second Bank of the United States (Old Customs House), Philadelphia (Pa.). 1818–24. *Façade* (Andrews)

473 SIR CHARLES BARRY and A. WELBY PUGIN. Houses of Parliament, London (England). Begun 1835. *Exterior* (NBR)

474 RICHARD UPJOHN. Trinity Church, New York (N.Y.). 1839–46. *Façade* (Andrews)

475 HENRI LABROUSTE. Bibliothèque Ste. Geneviève, Paris (France). 1843–50. *Reading Room* (Marburg)

475 BARON GEORGES EUGÈNE HAUSSMANN. Project for Modernizing the Street Plan of Paris. 1853. *Plan* (courtesy Institute of Fine Arts, N.Y.)

476 CHARLES GARNIER. The Opéra, Paris (France). 1861–74. *Façade and Grand Staircase* (Giraudon; H. Roger-Viollet)

477 CHARLES GARNIER. The Opéra, Paris (France). 1861–74. *Plan and Section* (Hitchcock, fig. 15)

478 HENRY HOBSON RICHARDSON. Sever Hall, Harvard University, Cambridge (Mass.). 1817–80. *Exterior* (Andrews)

478 MCKIM, MEADE & WHITE. Public Library, Boston (Mass.). 1888–92. *Exterior* (Andrews)

479 CHARLES F. A. VOYSEY. Broadleys, Lake Windermere (England). 1898. *Exterior* (Sanderson and Dixon)

479 HENRY HOBSON RICHARDSON. Stoughton House, Cambridge (Mass.). 1882–83. *Exterior* (G. W. Sheldon, *Artistic Country Seats*, I, N.Y., 1886)

480 SIR JOSEPH PAXTON. Crystal Palace II, Sydenham (England). 1852–54. *Air View, and View from Central Transept* (Fox; Gernsheim)

481 JOHN ROEBLING and WASHINGTON ROEBLING. Brooklyn Bridge, New York (N.Y.). 1869–83. *View* (Dept. of Public Works, N.Y.C.)

481 FERDINAND DUTERT. Galerie des Machines, International Exposition, Paris (France). 1889. *Interior* (Chevojon)

482 GUSTAVE EIFFEL. Eiffel Tower, Paris (France). 1887–89. *View* (Giraudon)

483 HENRY HOBSON RICHARDSON. Marshall Field Wholesale Store, Chicago (Ill.). 1885–87. *Exterior* (Chicago Archit. Photo Co.)

483 D. H. BURNHAM and J. W. ROOT. Reliance Building, Chicago (Ill.). 1890–94. *Exterior* (Chicago Archit. Photo Co.)

484 LOUIS SULLIVAN. Wainwright Building, St. Louis (Mo.). 1890–91. *Exterior* (Nickel)

485 LOUIS SULLIVAN. Carson Pirie Scott & Company, Store, Chicago (Ill.). 1899–1906. *Exterior and Window Detail* (Nickel)

page 486 CHARLES RENNIE MACKINTOSH. School of Art, Glasgow (Scotland). 1898–99. *Exterior* (Annan, Glasgow)

486 HECTOR GUIMARD. Métropolitain Station, Place de l'Étoile, Paris (France). 1900. *Exterior* (Stoedtner)

27. NINETEENTH-CENTURY ARCHITECTURE IN AUSTRIA, BELGIUM, GERMANY, ITALY, AND HOLLAND

487 GIUSEPPE MENGONI. Galleria Vittorio Emanuele, Milan (Italy). 1865–77. *Interior* (Alinari)

488 GIUSEPPE FRIZZI and CARLO PROMIS. Piazza Vittorio Veneto, Turin (Italy). Begun 1818. *View and Plan* (Alinari; *Alcuni Giorni in Torino*, 1842)

489 KARL F. VON SCHINKEL. Schauspielhaus, Berlin (Germany). 1819–21. *Façade* (DKV)

489 LEO VON KLENZE. Valhalla, Regensburg (Germany). 1830–42. *Exterior* (DKV)

490 LUDWIG PERSIUS. Friedenskirche, Potsdam (Germany). 1845–48. *View* (Hagemann, Berlin)

491 HEINRICH VON FERSTEL. Votivkirche, Vienna (Austria). 1856–79. *East Façade* (Ledermann, Vienna)

492 HENDRICK P. BERLAGE. Stock Exchange, Amsterdam (Holland). 1898. *Interior* (Sibbelee)

492 VICTOR HORTA. House at 4, Avenue Palmerson, Brussels (Belgium). 1894. *Entrance Hall* (courtesy The Museum of Modern Art, N.Y.)

493 VICTOR HORTA. Maison du Peuple, Brussels (Belgium). 1897. *Auditorium* (Kunstgewerbe Museum, Zurich)

28. TWENTIETH-CENTURY ARCHITECTURE

494 ANTONIO GAUDÍ. Casa Milá, Barcelona (Spain). 1905–7. *Chimney Detail* (Andrews)

495 ANTONIO GAUDÍ. Casa Milá, Barcelona (Spain). 1905–7. *Exterior and Floor Plan* (Mas; Hitchcock, fig. 35)

496 OTTO WAGNER. Post Office Savings Bank, Vienna (Austria). 1904–6. *Façade* (B.O.N.)

496 RAGNAR ÖSTBERG. City Hall, Stockholm (Sweden). 1909–23. *Exterior* (Hernried, Stockholm)

497 JOSEPH HOFFMANN. Palais Stoclet, Brussels (Belgium). 1905–11. *Street Façade* (Stoedtner)

497 JOSEPH M. OLBRICH. Wedding Tower (Hochzeitsturm), Darmstadt (Germany). 1907. *View* (Benevolo)

498 ADOLF LOOS. Steiner House, Vienna (Austria). 1910. *Garden Façade*

498 PETER BEHRENS. A.E.G. Turbine Factory, Berlin (Germany). 1909. *Exterior* (Marburg)

499 FRANK LLOYD WRIGHT. Robie House, Chicago (Ill.). 1909–10. *Exterior and Plans* (Engdahl, Hedrich–Blessing, Chicago)

500 ROBERT MAILLART. Tavanasa Bridge (Switzerland). 1905. *View* (courtesy Prof. Max Bill)

501 HENRY VAN DE VELDE. Theater for Werkbund Exhibition, Cologne (Germany). 1914. *Exterior* (Kröller-Müller Museum, Otterlo)

502 HENRY VAN DE VELDE. Theater for Werkbund Exhibition, Cologne (Germany). 1914. *Plan*

502 ERICH MENDELSOHN. Einstein Tower, Neubabelsberg (near Berlin, Germany). 1921. *Exterior* (German Information Center, N.Y.)

503 EUGÈNE FREYSSINET. Hangar, Orly Airport, Paris (France). 1916. *Exterior* (Arch. Phot.)

504 ANTONIO SANT'ELIA. Drawing of Power Station for The New City. 1914–16. *Museo Civico, Como*

504 WILLIS POLK. Hallidie Building, San Francisco (Cal.). 1918. *Façade* (Moulin Studios, San Francisco)

505 HANS POELZIG. Grosses Schauspielhaus, Berlin (Germany). 1919. *Auditorium* (Marburg)

506 AUGUSTE PERRET. Notre Dame, Le Raincy (near Paris, France). 1922–23. *Interior* (Kidder Smith)

507 GERRIT RIETVELD. Schröder House, Utrecht (Holland). 1924. *Exterior and Plans* (Jan Versnel, Amsterdam)

508 J. J. P. OUD. Workers' Houses, Hook of Holland (Holland). 1926–27. *Street Front* (courtesy The Museum of Modern Art, N.Y.)

page 508 J. A. BRINKMAN and L. C. VAN DER VLUGT. Van Nelle Factory, Rotterdam (Holland). 1927. *Exterior* (E. M. van Ojen, The Hague)

509 W. M. DUDOK. Town Hall, Hilversum (Holland). 1928–32. *Exterior* (C. A. Deul)

509 WALTER GROPIUS. The Bauhaus, Dessau (Germany). 1925–26. *General Plan*

510 WALTER GROPIUS. The Bauhaus, Dessau (Germany). 1925–26. *Machine Shop* (courtesy The Museum of Modern Art, N.Y.)

511 LUDWIG MIES VAN DER ROHE. German Pavilion, International Exposition, Barcelona (Spain). 1929. *Plan and View* (courtesy The Museum of Modern Art, N. Y.; Williams & Meyer)

512 LE CORBUSIER. Savoie House, Poissy (France). 1929–30. *Exterior and Interior* (Hervé)

513 GEORGE HOWE and WILLIAM LESCAZE. Philadelphia Savings Fund Society Building, Philadelphia (Pa.). 1931–32. *Exterior* (Ben Schnall, N.Y.)

514 HENDRICK P. BERLAGE. Gemeentemuseum, The Hague (Holland). 1934. *Exterior* (Benevolo)

514 GUNNAR ASPLUND. Woodland Crematorium, Stockholm (Sweden). 1935–40. *Entrance* (Hernried, Stockholm)

515 FRANK LLOYD WRIGHT. Kaufmann House, "Falling Waters," Bear Run (near Pittsburgh, Pa.). 1936–39. *Exterior* (Hedrich–Blessing, Chicago)

516 FRANK LLOYD WRIGHT. Johnson Wax Building, Racine (Wis.). 1936–39. *View* (courtesy S. C. Johnson & Son, Inc.)

517 LUCIO DE COSTA, OSCAR NIEMEYER, and others. Ministry of Education and Health, Rio de Janeiro (Brazil). 1937–43. *Façade* (Kidder Smith)

518 LE CORBUSIER. Unité d'Habitation, Marseilles (France). 1947–52. *View of Recreation Area on Roof and Exterior* (Kidder Smith)

519 AUGUSTE PERRET. Place de l'Hôtel de Ville, Le Havre (France). 1948–54. *View* (Chevojon)

520 WALLACE K. HARRISON and International Advisory Committee. United Nations Buildings (N.Y.). 1949–61. *General View* (courtesy United Nations)

521 ELIEL SAARINEN and EERO SAARINEN. Christ Lutheran Church, Minneapolis (Min.). 1949–50. *Interior* (G. M. Ryan)

522 PIER LUIGI NERVI. Exhibition Hall, Turin (Italy). 1948–50. *Interior* (Moncalvo)

523 LUDWIG MIES VAN DER ROHE. Lake Shore Drive Apartments, Chicago (Ill.). 1950–52. *General View* (Hedrich–Blessing, Chicago)

523 SKIDMORE, OWINGS & MERRILL. Lever House, New York (N.Y.). 1952. *Exterior* (Ezra Stoller)

524 ALVAR AALTO. Civic Center, Säynätsalo (Finland). 1950–51. *Courtyard* (E. Mäkinen, Helsinki)

524 VAN DEN BROEK and BAKEMA. The Lijnbaan, Rotterdam (Holland). 1951–53. *Plan (Town Planning Review*, XXVII, p. 23)

525 LE CORBUSIER. Chapel of Notre Dame du Haut, Ronchamp (France). 1950–55. *Exterior and Isometric Diagram* (Hervé)

526 LE CORBUSIER. Chapel of Notre Dame du Haut, Ronchamp (France). 1950–55. *Interior* (Hervé)

527 LE CORBUSIER. City of Chandigarh (Punjab, India). 1951. *General Plan.* (Le Corbusier, *L'Œuvre Complète,* VI)

527 LUCIO DE COSTA. City of Brasília (Federal District, Goiás, Brazil). 1957. *General Plan*

528 SKIDMORE, OWINGS & MERRILL. Union Carbide Building, New York (N.Y.). 1963. *Exterior* (courtesy Union Carbide Corp.)

529 I. M. PEI. Earth Sciences Center, Massachusetts Institute of Technology, Cambridge (Mass.). 1963. *Exterior* (Bichajian)

THE MODERN WORLD

26. Nineteenth-Century Architecture in England, France, and the United States of America

CHARLES PERCIER and PIERRE F. L. FONTAINE. Rue de Rivoli,
Paris (France). 1802–55. *View toward the west*

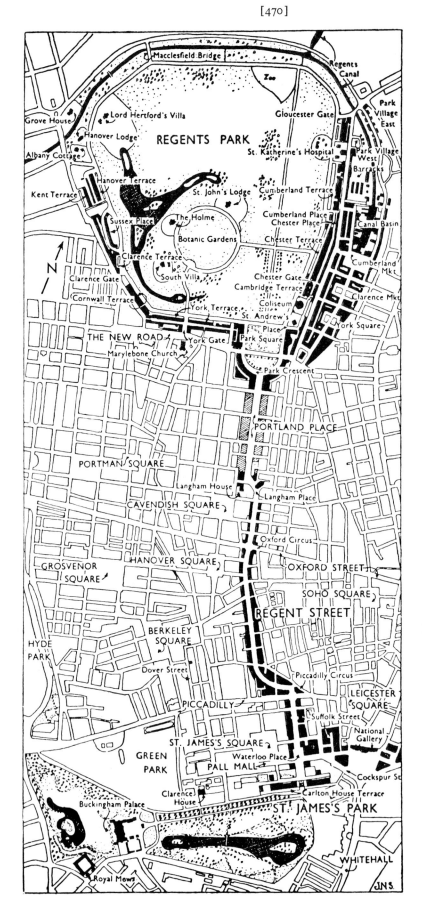

JOHN NASH.
Regent Street,
London (England).
1811–35. *Plan*

JOHN NASH. The Royal Pavilion, Brighton (England).
Remodeled 1815–18. *Center portion of East Façade*

SIR ROBERT SMIRKE. British Museum, London (England).
Begun 1824. *View of South Façade*

BENJAMIN LATROBE. Catholic Cathedral, Baltimore (Md.). Begun 1805.
Exterior View from southwest, and Interior View toward the northeast

WILLIAM STRICKLAND. Second Bank of the United States (Old Customs House),
Philadelphia (Pa.). 1818–24. *View of Façade from southeast*

SIR CHARLES BARRY and A. WELBY PUGIN. Houses of Parliament, London
(England). Begun 1835. *View of Exterior from northeast*

RICHARD UPJOHN.
Trinity Church,
New York (N.Y.).
1839–46. *View of
Façade from the east*

HENRI LABROUSTE. Bibliothèque Ste. Geneviève, Paris (France).
1843–50. *Interior of Reading Room*

BARON GEORGES EUGÈNE HAUSSMANN. Project for Modernizing the
Street Plan of Paris. 1853. *Plan (after Alfred Armand)*

CHARLES GARNIER.
The Opéra, Paris
(France). 1861–74.
*View of Façade,
and Upper Flight of
Grand Staircase*

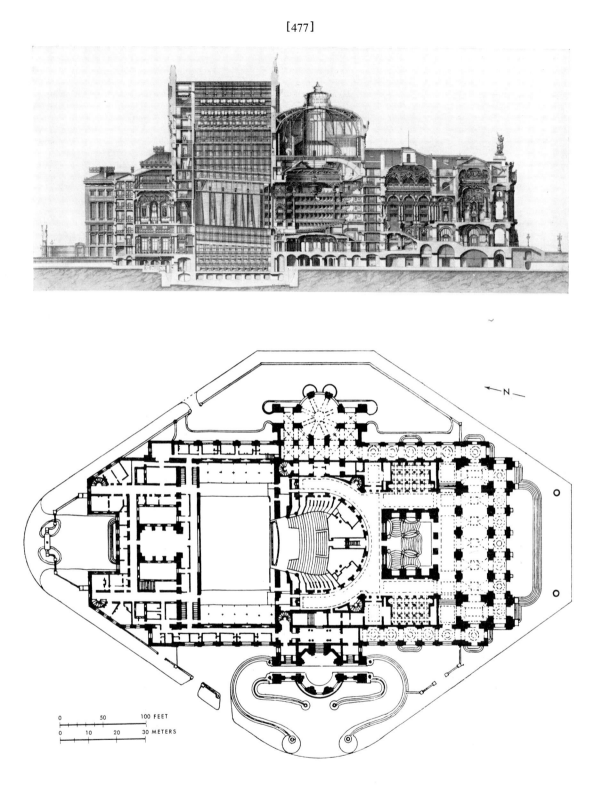

CHARLES GARNIER. The Opéra, Paris (France). 1861–74.
Plan and Longitudinal Section

HENRY HOBSON RICHARDSON. Sever Hall, Harvard University, Cambridge
(Mass.). 1817–80. *View of Exterior from the west*

MCKIM, MEADE & WHITE (architectural firm). Public Library, Boston
(Mass.). 1888–92. *View of Exterior from the east*

CHARLES F. A. VOYSEY. Broadleys, Lake Windermere (England).
1898. *View of Exterior from southwest*

HENRY HOBSON RICHARDSON. Stoughton House, Cambridge (Mass.).
1882–83. *View of Exterior from southwest (contemporary photograph)*

SIR JOSEPH PAXTON. Crystal Palace II, Sydenham (England). 1852–54. *Air View, and View from Central Transept toward North Transept (contemporary photograph)*

JOHN ROEBLING and WASHINGTON ROEBLING. Brooklyn Bridge,
New York (N.Y.). 1869–83. *View from the east*

FERDINAND DUTERT. Galerie des Machines, International
Exposition, Paris (France). 1889. *View of Interior*

GUSTAVE EIFFEL.
Eiffel Tower,
Paris (France).
1887–89.
General View

D. H. Burnham and J. W. Root. Reliance Building,
Chicago (Ill.). 1890–94. *View of Exterior*

Henry Hobson Richardson. Marshall Field Wholesale Store,
Chicago (Ill.). 1885–87 (demolished 1930). *View of Exterior*

Louis Sullivan. Wainwright Building, St. Louis (Mo.).
1890–91. *View of Exterior from southeast*

LOUIS SULLIVAN.
Carson Pirie Scott &
Company Store,
Chicago (Ill.). 1899;
extended 1903–4, 1906.
*View of Exterior
toward southeast,
and Window Detail*

RIGHT
CHARLES RENNIE MACKINTOSH.
School of Art, Glasgow
(Scotland). 1898–99. *View of
Exterior from northwest*

BELOW
HECTOR GUIMARD.
Métropolitain Station,
Place de l'Étoile,
Paris (France). 1900 (now
demolished). *Exterior View*

THE MODERN WORLD

27. Nineteenth-Century Architecture in Austria, Belgium, Germany, Italy, and Holland

GIUSEPPE MENGONI. Galleria Vittorio Emanuele,
Milan (Italy). 1865–77. *View of Interior*

GIUSEPPE FRIZZI and CARLO PROMIS. Piazza Vittorio Veneto, Turin (Italy).
Begun 1818. *View toward southeast (Church of Gran Madre di Dio
by* FERDINANDO BONSIGNORE, *1818–31). and General Plan*

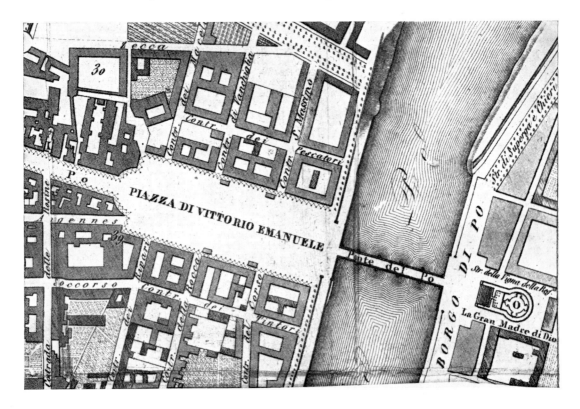

KARL F. VON SCHINKEL. Schauspielhaus, Berlin
(Germany). 1819–21. *View of Façade*

LEO VON KLENZE. Valhalla, Regensburg (Germany).
1830–42. *General View of Exterior*

LUDWIG PERSIUS. Friedenskirche, Potsdam (Germany).
1845–48. *General View from the east*

HEINRICH VON FERSTEL. Votivkirche, Vienna (Austria).
1856–79. *View of East Façade*

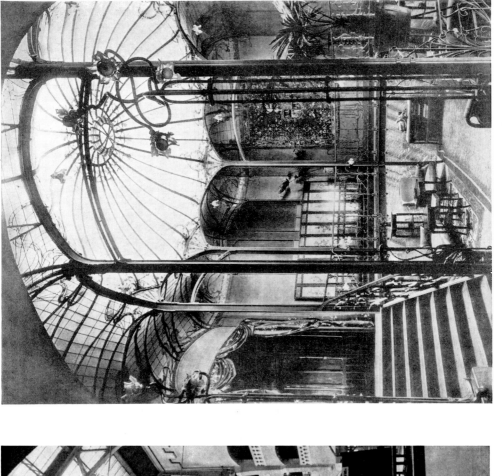

Victor Horta. House at 4, Avenue Palmerson, Brussels (Belgium). 1894. *Interior of Entrance Hall*

Hendrick P. Berlage. Stock Exchange, Amsterdam (Holland). 1898. *View of Interior*

VICTOR HORTA. Maison du Peuple, Brussels (Belgium). 1897. *Interior of Auditorium*

THE MODERN WORLD

28. *Twentieth-Century Architecture*

ANTONIO GAUDÍ. Casa Milá (apartment house),
Barcelona (Spain). 1905–7. *Chimney Detail*

ANTONIO GAUDÍ. Casa Milá (apartment house), Barcelona (Spain). 1905–7.
View of Exterior, and Plan of a Typical Floor

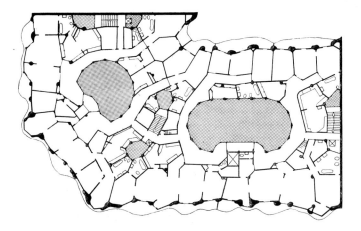

Oᴛᴛᴏ Wᴀɢɴᴇʀ. Post Office Savings Bank, Vienna (Austria). 1904–6. *View of Façade*

Rᴀɢɴᴀʀ Ösᴛʙᴇʀɢ. City Hall, Stockholm (Sweden). 1909–23. *View of Exterior*

ABOVE
JOSEPH HOFFMANN.
Palais Stoclet, Brussels
(Belgium). 1905–11.
View of Street Façade

RIGHT
JOSEPH M. OLBRICH.
Wedding Tower
(Hochzeitsturm),
Darmstadt (Germany).
1907. *General View*

ADOLF LOOS. Steiner House, Vienna (Austria). 1910. *View of Garden Façade*

PETER BEHRENS. A. E. G. Turbine Factory,
Berlin (Germany). 1909. *Exterior View*

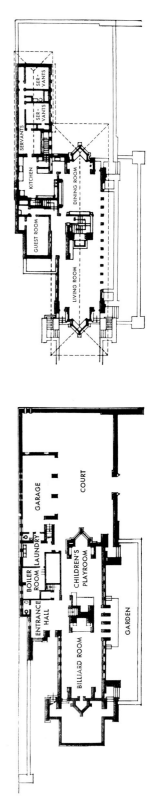

FRANK LLOYD WRIGHT. Robie House, Chicago (Ill.). 1909–10. *View of Exterior, and Plans of Ground Floor and First Floor*

ROBERT MAILLART.
Tavanasa Bridge over
Rhine River (Switzerland).
1905 (destroyed 1927).
General View

HENRY VAN DE VELDE. Theater for Werkbund Exhibition, Cologne (Germany). 1914. *Exterior View*

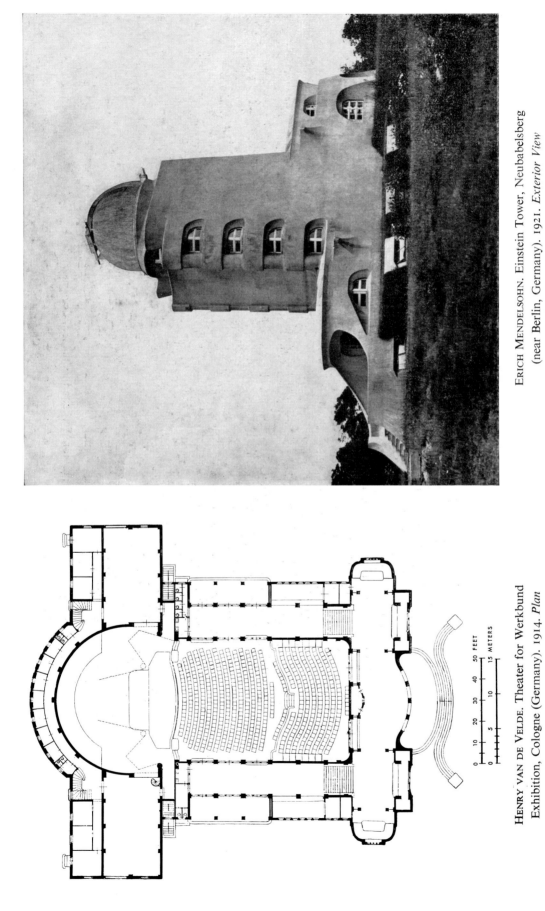

ERICH MENDELSOHN. Einstein Tower, Neubabelsberg
(near Berlin, Germany). 1921. *Exterior View*

HENRY VAN DE VELDE. Theater for Werkbund
Exhibition, Cologne (Germany). 1914. *Plan*

EUGÈNE FREYSSINET.
Hangar, Orly Airport,
Paris (France).
1916 (destroyed in
World War II).
View of Exterior

WILLIS POLK. Hallidie Building, San Francisco
(Cal.). 1918. *View of Façade*

ANTONIO SANT'ELIA. Power Station for The New City
(*Città Futura*). Drawing, 1914–16. *Museo Civico, Como*

HANS POELZIG. Grosses Schauspielhaus, Berlin (Germany).
1919. *Interior of Auditorium*

Auguste Perret. Notre Dame, Le Raincy (near Paris, France).
1922–23. *View of Interior toward the apse*

GERRIT RIETVELD. Schröder House,
Utrecht (Holland). 1924.
Exterior View, and
Plans of Three Floors

J. J. P. OUD. Workers' Houses, Hook of Holland (Holland).
1926–27. *View of Street Front*

J. A. BRINKMAN and L. C. VAN DER VLUGT. Van Nelle Factory,
Rotterdam (Holland). 1927. *View of Exterior*

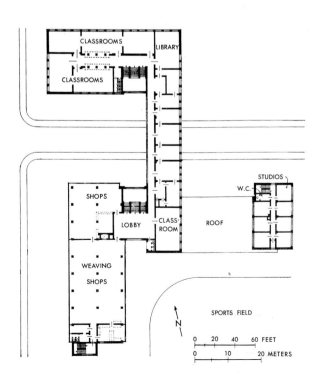

ABOVE

W. M. DUDOK. Town Hall,
Hilversum (Holland).
1928–32. *View of Exterior*

RIGHT

WALTER GROPIUS. The Bauhaus,
Dessau (Germany). 1925–26.
General Plan of First Floor
(View on following page)

WALTER GROPIUS. The Bauhaus, Dessau (Germany). 1925–26. *Exterior View of Machine Shop (General Plan on preceding page)*

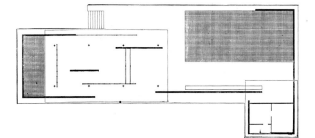

LUDWIG MIES VAN DER ROHE. German Pavilion, International Exposition, Barcelona (Spain). 1929. *Plan, and View from End of Court*

LE CORBUSIER. Savoie House, Poissy (France). 1929–30. *View of Exterior,
and Interior View of Living Room toward Terrace*

GEORGE HOWE and WILLIAM LESCAZE. Philadelphia Savings Fund Society
Building, Philadelphia (Pa.). 1931–32. *View of Exterior*

HENDRICK P. BERLAGE. Gemeentemuseum, The Hague
(Holland). 1934. *Exterior View*

GUNNAR ASPLUND. Woodland Crematorium, Stockholm
(Sweden). 1935–40. *View of Entrance*

Frank Lloyd Wright.
Kaufmann House,
"Falling Waters,"
Bear Run (near
Pittsburgh, Pa.).
1936–39. *Exterior View*

Frank Lloyd Wright. Johnson Wax Building, Racine (Wis.).
1936–39. *General View of Exterior*

LUCIO DE COSTA, OSCAR NIEMEYER, and others. Ministry of Education
and Health, Rio de Janeiro (Brazil). 1937–43. *Entrance and Façade*

Le Corbusier. Unité d'Habitation (apartment house), Marseilles
(France). 1947–52. *View of Recreation Area on Roof, and Exterior*

AUGUSTE PERRET. Place de l'Hôtel de Ville, Le Havre (France). 1948–54.
View from southeast

WALLACE K. HARRISON and International Advisory Committee (LE CORBUSIER, NIEMEYER, and others). United Nations Buildings (N.Y.). 1949–61.
View from above toward the north, including Memorial Library, Secretariat Building, and Assembly Buildings

ELIEL SAARINEN and EERO SAARINEN. Christ Lutheran Church, Minneapolis
(Minn.). 1949–50. *View of Interior toward the east*

PIER LUIGI NERVI. Exhibition Hall, Turin (Italy). 1948–50. *Portion of Interior*

SKIDMORE, OWINGS & MERRILL (architectural firm). Lever House,
New York (N.Y.). 1952. *View of Exterior from southeast*

LUDWIG MIES VAN DER ROHE. Lake Shore Drive Apartments,
Chicago (Ill.). 1950–52. *General View from southwest*

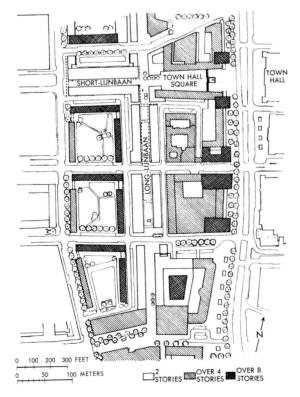

SHORT-LIJNBAAN

TOWN HALL SQUARE

TOWN HALL

LONG-LIJNBAAN

N

0   100   200   300 FEET
0   50   100 METERS

☐ 2 STORIES   ▨ OVER 4 STORIES   ◼ OVER 8 STORIES

ABOVE
ALVAR AALTO. Civic Center,
Säynätsalo (Finland). 1950–51.
View of Courtyard from the west

LEFT
VAN DEN BROEK and BAKEMA
(architectural firm).
The Lijnbaan, Rotterdam (Holland).
1951–53. *Plan of General Area*

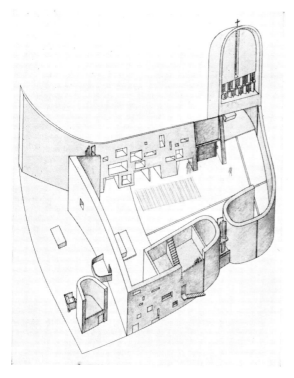

LE CORBUSIER.
Chapel of Notre Dame du Haut,
Ronchamp (France).
1950–55. *View of Exterior
from southeast, and
Isometric Diagram*

Le Corbusier. Chapel of Notre Dame du Haut, Ronchamp (France). 1950–55.
View of Interior toward southwest

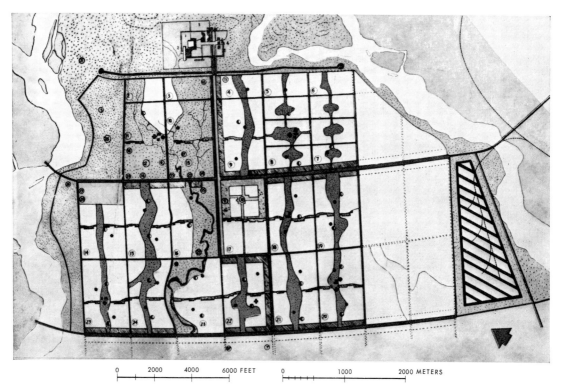

LE CORBUSIER. City of Chandigarh (Punjab, India). 1951. *General Plan*

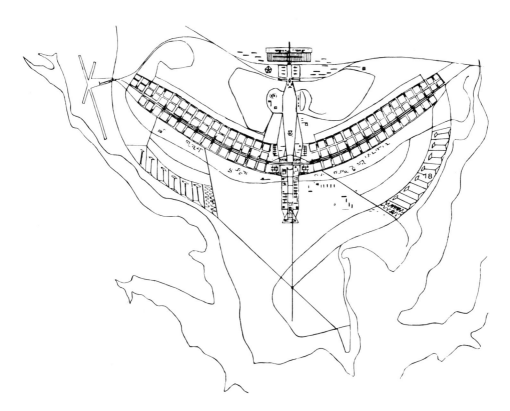

LUCIO DE COSTA. City of Brasília (Federal District, Goiás, Brazil). 1957. *General Plan*

SKIDMORE, OWINGS & MERRILL (architectural firm). Union Carbide Building,
New York (N.Y.). 1963. *View of Exterior from northeast*

I. M. Pei. Earth Sciences Center, Massachusetts Institute of Technology, Cambridge (Mass.). 1963. *Exterior View*

INDEX OF PERSONS AND PLACES

Names of architects are in CAPITALS; names of locations are in roman;
page numbers are in *italic*. Buildings are listed according to location.

A

Aachen (Germany), Palace of Charlemagne, *197–99*
AALTO, ALVAR (b. 1898), *524*
ADAM, ROBERT (1728–92) *443*
Agra (India), Taj Mahal, *160*
Aigues-Mortes (France), Ramparts, *246*
Ajantā (India), Cave No. 19, *164*
ALBERTI, LEONE BATTISTA (1402–72), *309–10, 313–15*
Albi (France), Cathedral of Ste. Cécile, *260–61*
Amiens (France), Cathedral, *238–40*
AMMANATI, BARTOLOMMEO (1511–92), *341*
Amsterdam (Holland), Stock Exchange, *492*
Anet (France), Château of, *361*
Angkor (Cambodia), Shrine of Angkor Wat, *166*
Annaberg (Germany), St. Anne, *277*
ANTHEMIUS OF TRALLES (fl. 6th century A.D.), *138–41*
Antwerp (Belgium), Museum of Fine Arts; *St. Barbara* by JAN VAN EYCK, *245*
Apulia (Italy), Castel del Monte, *255*
ASAM, COSMAS DAMIAN (1686–1739), *453*
ASAM, EGID QUIRIN (1692–1750) *453*
ASPLUND, GUNNAR (1885–1940), *514*
Athens (Greece): Agora, *64, 65, 77*; Erechtheum, *72–74*; General Plan, *64*; Olympieion, *76*; Parthenon, *67–68*; *Pen Drawing of Acropolis, 74*; Propylaea, *69–71*; South Slope of Acropolis, *66*; Temple of Athena Nike, *70*; Theater of Dionysus, *66*; "Theseum," *75*
Augsburg (Germany), Town Hall, *369–70*
Autun (France), Cathedral of St. Lazare, *219*
Avignon (France), Pont St. Bénezet, *246*

B

Baalbek (Lebanon), Temples, *98–100*

Babylon (Iraq), Ishtar Gate, *45*
Baltimore (Md.), Catholic Cathedral, *472*
Barcelona (Spain): Casa Milá, *494–95*; International Exposition, *511*
BARRY, SIR CHARLES (1795–1860), *473*
Bassae (Greece), Temple of Apollo, *77–78*
Bath (England), Circus and Royal Crescent, *442*
Bear Run (near Pittsburgh, Pa.), Kaufmann House, *515*
Beauvais (France), Cathedral, *241–42*
BECERRA, FRANCISCO (d. 1605), *367*
BEHRENS, PETER (1868–1938), *498*
BERLAGE, HENDRICK P. (1856–1934), *492, 514*
Berlin (Germany): Grosses Schauspielhaus, *505*; Royal Palace, *413*; Schauspielhaus, *489*; A.E.G. Turbine Factory, *498*
BERNINI, GIAN LORENZO (1598–1680), *376, 386–88, 399*
Bethlehem (Jordan), Church of the Nativity, *123*
Bhuvaneshwar (India), Great Temple Compound, *165*
Blois (France), Château of, *355*
BÖBLINGER, MATTHÄUS (fl. 2nd half 15th century), *276*
BOFFRAND, GERMAIN (1667–1754), *437*
Borobudur (Indonesia), Sanctuary, *166*
BORROMINI, FRANCESCO (1599–1667), *380–84*
Boscoreale (Italy), *Wall Painting, 111*
Boston (Mass.), Public Library, *478*
Bourges (France), House of Jacques Cœur, *266*
Brà (Italy), S. Chiara, *434–35*
BRAMANTE, DONATO (1444–1514), *319–21, 323–27, 331–32*
Brasília (Brazil), City Plan, *527*
BRETON, GILLES LE (fl. 1528–40), *358–59*
Brighton (England), Royal Pavilion, *471*
BRINKMAN, J. A. (b. 1902), *508*

BROSSE, SALOMON DE (c. 1562–1626), *364*
BRUNELLESCHI, FILIPPO (1377–1446), *282–84, 301–06*
Brussels (Belgium), House at 4, Ave. Palmerson, *492*; Maison du Peuple, *493*; Palais Stoclet, *497*
BURLINGTON, EARL OF (1694–1753), *444*
BURNHAM, D. H. (1846–1912), *483*

C

Caen (France): St. Etienne, *214–15*; St. Pierre, *360*
Cairo (Egypt), Madrasa of Sultan Hasan, *155*
CAMBIO, ARNOLFO DI (1232–1301), *282*
Cambridge (England), King's College Chapel, *272–73*
Cambridge (Mass.): Earth Sciences Center, M.I.T., *529*; Sever Hall, Harvard Univ., *478*; Stoughton House, *479*
CAMPEN, JACOB VAN (1595–1657), *420*
CARATTI, FRANCESCO (d. 1617), *412*
Carnac (France), Dolmen, *17*
Caserta (Italy), Royal Palace, *432–33*
Cerveteri (Italy), Tomb of the Reliefs, *88*
Chambord (France), Château of, *356–57*
Chan-Chan (Peru), *185*
Chandigarh (India), City Plan, *525*
Charlottesville (Va.), Monticello, *463*
Chartres (France), Cathedral, *237*
Chicago (Ill.): Carson Pirie Scott & Co. Store, *485*; Lake Shore Drive Apartments, *523*; Marshall Field Wholesale Store, *483*; Reliance Building, *483*; Robie House, *499*
Chichén Itzá (Mexico): Plan, *184*; Pyramid and Temple, *183*
Classe (Italy), S. Apollinare *130–31*
Cluny (France), Third Abbey Church and Monastery, *213*
CODUCCI, MAURO (c. 1440–1504), *322*

Cologne (Germany): St. Mary in Capitol, *228–29*; Werkbund Exhibition, *501–02*

Cordova (Spain), Mosque, *151–52*

CORTONA, DOMENICO DA (1495–1549), *356–57*

CORTONA, PIETRO DA (1596–1669), *378–79, 385*

COSTA, LÚCIO DE (b. 1902), *517, 527*

COYSEVOX, ANTOINE (1640–1720), *402*

Ctesiphon (Iraq), Sassanian Palace, *49*

Cuzco (Peru): Cathedral, *367, 421*; La Merced, *421*

D

Daigoji (Japan), Pagoda, *169*

Darmstadt (Germany), Wedding Tower, *497*

DE CORNY, EMMANUEL HÉRÉ (1705–63), *438*

Deir el Bahari (Egypt): Funerary Temple of Queen Hatshepsut, *31–33*; Mentuhotep Temple, *27*

Delos (Greece), House Plans, *82*

Delphi (Greece): Athenian Treasury, *63*; Siphnian Treasury, *62*

Dessau (Germany), Bauhaus *509–10*

Didyma (Turkey), Temple of Apollo, *79–80*

Dresden (Germany), Zwinger, *452*

DUDOK, W. M. (b. 1884), *509*

Durham (England), Cathedral, *226–27*

Dur-Untash (Iran), Elamite Ziggurat, *42*

DUTERT, FERDINAND (1845–1906), *481*

E

Edfu (Egypt), Temple of Horus, *39*

EIFFEL, GUSTAVE (1832–1923), *482*

Ely (England), Cathedral, *268*

ENGELBERG, BURKHARD (fl. c. 1500), *279*

Epidaurus (Greece): Theater, *85*; Tholos, Plan, *84*

ERLACH, JOHANN FISCHER VON (1656–1723), *416–18, 449–50*

Escorial (Spain): City of, *365*; Church, *366*

Exeter (England), Cathedral, *267*

F

FERSTEL, HEINRICH VON (1828–83), *491*

FISCHER, JOHANN MICHAEL (1692–1766), *456–57*

FISCHER VON ERLACH, *see* ERLACH, JOHANN FISCHER VON

Florence (Italy): Campanile, *285*; Cathedral (S. Maria del Fiore), *283–84*; Foundling Hospital, *301*; Laurentian Library, *336*; Palazzo Medici-Riccardi, *307–08*; Palazzo Rucellai, *309*; Palazzo Vecchio, *257*; S. Croce, *254* (Pazzi Chapel, *304–05*); S. Lorenzo, *302–303*; S. Maria degli Angeli, *305*; S. Spirito, *306*; Uffizi, *342*

FONTAINE, PIERRE F. L. (1762–1853), *469*

Fontainebleau (France), Château of, *358–59*

FONTANA, DOMENICO (1543–1607), *353*

Fossanova (Italy), Abbey Church, *251–52*

FREYSSINET, EUGÈNE (b.1879), *503*

FRIZZI, GIUSEPPE (1797–1831), *488*

FUGA, FERDINANDO (1699–1780), *427, 430*

G

Gabel (Czechoslovakia), St. Lawrence, *414–15*

GABRIEL, JACQUES ANGE (1667–1742), *439*

GALILEI, ALESSANDRO (1691–1737), *427*

GARNIER, CHARLES (1825–98), *476–77*

GAUDÍ, ANTONIO (1852–1926), *494–95*

Gerona (Spain), Cathedral, *280*

GIBBS, JAMES (1683–1774), *442*

Giza (Egypt), Pyramids, *25–27*

Glasgow (Scotland), School of Art, *486*

Gloucester (England), Cathedral, *269–70*

Gmünd, Schwäbisch (Germany), Church of the Holy Cross, *274*

Granada (Spain): Alhambra Palace, *153–54*; Cartuja, *459*; Cathedral, *364*; Palace of Charles V, *363*

GREGORINI, DOMENICO (1700–77), *428*

GROPIUS, WALTER (b. 1883), *509–10*

GUARINI, GUARINO (1624–83), *389–92*

GUIDETTI, GUIDO (d. 1564), *345*

GUIMARD, HECTOR (1867–1942), *486*

H

Hague, The (Holland): Gemeentemuseum, *514*; Mauritshuis, *420*

Hal Tarxien (Malta), Temple, *19*

Hampton Court (England), Palace, *409*

HARDOUIN-MANSART, JULES (1646–1708), *400–402, 406–07*

HARRISON, PETER (1716–75), *461*

HARRISON, WALLACE K. (b. 1895), *520*

Hattusas (Turkey), Lion Gate, *46*

HAUSSMANN, BARON GEORGES EUGÈNE (1809–91), *475*

Herculaneum (Italy), House of Neptune and Amphitrite, *110*

HERRERA, JUAN DE (c. 1530–97), *365–66*

HESIUS, WILLIAM (born c. 1600), *419*

HILDEBRANDT, JOHANN LUKAS VON (1688–1745), *414–15, 451*

Hildesheim (Germany), St. Michael, *202–03*

Hilversum (Holland), Town Hall, *509*

HOFFMANN, JOSEPH (1870–1956), *497*

HOLL, ELIAS (1593–1646), *369–70*

HONNECOURT, VILLARD DE (fl. 13th century), *244*

Hook of Holland (Holland), Workers' Houses, *508*

HORTA, VICTOR (1861–1947), *492–93*

Horyuji (Japan), Monastery, *170*

HOWE, GEORGE (1886–1954), *513*

Hyogo (Japan), Himeji Castle, *176*

I

ICTINUS (5th century B.C.), *67–68*

Ingelheim (Germany), Palace of Charlemagne, *196*

Ise (Japan), Sanctuary, *167*

Isfahan (Iran): Farahabad Gardens, *161*; Maidan-i-Shah, *156*; Masjid-i-Jami, *156–57*

ISIDORUS OF MILETUS (fl. 6th century A.D.), *138–41*

Istanbul (Turkey): Hagia Sophia, *138–41*; Mosque of Ahmed I, *159*; SS. Sergius and Bacchus, *136–37*

J

JEANNERET, CHARLES-EDOUARD, *see* LE CORBUSIER

JEFFERSON, THOMAS (1743–1826), *463*

JONES, INIGO (1573–1652), *408*

JUVARRA, FILIPPO (1678–1736), *423–26*

K

Kansas City (Mo.), Museum, Han Dynasty House, *168*

Karnak (Egypt): Festival Hall of Tuthmosis III, *29*; Pylon of Tuthmosis I, *30*; Temple of Amun, *29–30, 38*

KENT, WILLIAM (c. 1685–1748), *444*

Khorsabad (Iraq): City Plan, *43*; Citadel of Sargon II, *44*

KLENZE, LEOPOLD VON (1784–1864), *489*

Knossos (Crete), Palace of Minos, *52–53*

Kyoto (Japan): Katsura Imperial Palace, *178*; Kuroshoin, Nishi Honganji, *178*

L

Labná (Mexico), Palace and Temple, *182*
LABROUSTE, HENRI (1801–75), *475*
Lagash (Iraq), *Gudea with Architectural Plan* (Louvre), *41*
Lake Windermere (England), Broadleys, *479*
LATROBE, BENJAMIN H. (1764–1820), *472*
LE CORBUSIER (CHARLES EDOUARD JEANNERET), (b. 1887), *512, 518, 520, 525–27*
Le Havre (France), Place de l'Hôtel de Ville, *519*
LE NÔTRE, ANDRÉ (1613–1700), *403–04*
Le Raincy (France), Notre Dame, *506*
LE VAU, LOUIS (1612–70), *398, 399b–401*
LEBRUN, CHARLES (1619–90), *402*
LEMERCIER, JACQUES (1585–1654), *395–96*
L'ENFANT, PIERRE CHARLES (1754–1825), *464*
Leptis Magna (Libya), Basilica, *105*
LESCAZE, WILLIAM (b. 1896), *513*
LESCOT, PIERRE (c. 1510–78), *362*
LI JUNG-CHIN (Yüan Dynasty, 1260–1368), *175*
LIGORIO, PIRRO (c. 1520–80), *340*
London (England): British Museum, *471*; Chiswick House, *444*; Home House, *443*; House in the Adelphi, *443*; Houses of Parliament, *473*; Regent Street, *470*; St. Martin's-in-the-Fields, *442*; St. Paul's, *409–10*; Whitehall Palace, *408*
LONGHENA, BALDASSARE (1592–1682), *377*
L'ORME, PHILIBERT DE (c. 1512–70), *359, 361*
LOOS, ADOLF (1870–1933), *498*
Lorsch (Germany), Gatehouse, Monastery, *195*
Louvain (Belgium), St. Michel, *419*
LUKAS VON HILDEBRANDT, *see* HILDEBRANDT, JOHANN LUKAS VON
Luxor (Egypt), Temple of Amen-Mut-Khonsu, *36–37*

M

Machu Picchu (Peru), Citadel, *186–87*
MACHUCA, PEDRO (fl. 1517–50), *363*
McINTYRE, SAMUEL (1757–1811), *463*
McKIM, MEAD & WHITE (architectural firm), *478*

MACKINTOSH, CHARLES RENNIE (1868–1928), *486*
MADERNO, CARLO (1556–1629), *373–76*
MAILLART, ROBERT (1872–1940), *500*
Maisons (France), Château of, *397*
MAITANI, LORENZO (before 1275–1330), *286*
Malthi (Greece), Plan of Helladic Town, *51*
MANSART, FRANÇOIS (1598–1666), *395–97*
Mantua (Italy): Palazzo del Tè, *336*; S. Andrea, *313–15*
Marseilles (France), Unité d'Habitation, *518*
Marzabotto (Italy), City Plan, *86*
MEISSONIER, JUSTE AURÉLE (1693–1750), *436*
Melk (Austria), Benedictine Abbey, *447–48*
MENDELSOHN, ERICH (1887–1953), *502*
MENGONI, GIUSEPPE (1829–77), *487*
Mesa Verde (Col.), Cliff Dwellings, *22*
MICHELANGELO BUONARROTI (1474–1564), *333–36, 338–39, 343–44*
MICHELOZZO DI BARTOLOMMEO (1396–1472), *307–308*
MIES VAN DER ROHE, LUDWIG (b. 1886), *511, 523*
Milan (Italy): Cathedral of, *287–89*; Galleria Vittorio Emanuele, *487*; S. Ambrogio *211–12*; S. Lorenzo Maggiore, *133*; S. Maria delle Grazie, *320–21*; S. Maria presso S. Satiro, *319*
Miletus (Turkey): City Plan, *81*; Market Gate, *119*
MILLER, WOLFGANG (fl. 2nd half 16th century), *368*
Minneapolis (Minn.), Christ Lutheran Church, *520*
MIQUE, RICHARD (1728–94), *441*
Mohenjo-Daro (Pakistan), Plan of a City Block, *50*
Moravia (Czechoslovakia), Schloss Frain, *416–17*
Moscow (U.S.S.R.), Cathedral of St. Basil, *144*
MNESICLES (5th century B.C.), *69–71*
Mshatta (Jordan), Palace, *150*
Münster (Germany), Town Hall, *278*
Munich (Germany), St. Michael, *368*
Murcia (Spain), Cathedral, *460*
Mycenae (Greece): Lion Gate, *56*; "Treasury of Atreus," *54*

N

Naksh-i-Rustam (Iran), Achaemenian Royal Tomb, *50*

Nancy (France), Place de la Carrière and Hemicycle, *438*
Nara (Japan), Kondo, Toshodaiji, *171*
NASH, JOHN (1752–1835), *470–71*
NERVI, PIER LUIGI (b. 1891), *522*
Neubabelsberg (Germany), Einstein Tower, *502*
NEUMANN, BALTHASAR (1687–1753), *454–55*
New Orleans (La.), Keller House, *462*
New York (N.Y.): Brooklyn Bridge, *481*; Lever House, *523*; Trinity Church, *474*; Union Carbide Bldg., *528*; United Nations Bldgs., *520*
Newport (R.I.), Brick Market, *461*
NIEMEYER, OSCAR (b. 1907), *517, 520*
Nîmes (France): Maison Carrée, *93*; Pont du Gard, *118*
Nivelles (Belgium), Ste. Gertrude, *204*
Northamptonshire (England): Burghley House, *372*; Earl's Barton, *205*
Northern Rhodesia (Africa), Ba Ila Village, *21*
Nottinghamshire (England), Wollaton Hall, *371*
Nuremberg (Germany), St. Sebald, *275*

O

OLBRICH, JOSEPH M. (1867–1908), *497*
Ollantaytambo (Peru), Masonry, *188*
Olynthus (Greece), Plan for Section of City, *82*
Orvieto (Italy), Cathedral, *286*
ÖSTBERG, RAGNAR (1866–1945), *496*
Ostia (Italy): Apartment House *112*; Harbor, *120*
Ottobeuren (Germany), Benedictine Abbey, *456–57*
OUD, J. J. P. (1890–1963), *508*
Oxfordshire (England), Blenheim Palace, *445–46*

P

Paestum (Italy): Air View and Plan, *58*; "Basilica," *57, 59*; "Temple of Poseidon", *57, 60–61*
PALLADIO, ANDREA (1508–80), *346–49*
Palmanova (Italy), Design of City, *354*
Paris (France): Bibliothèque Ste. Geneviève, *475*; Church of the Invalides, *406*; Eiffel Tower, *482*; Hôtel de Soubise, *437*; International Exposition, *481*; Louvre, *362, 399, 405*; Métropolitan Station, *486*; Notre Dame, *234–36*; Opéra, *476–77*; Orly Airport, *503*; Pan-

théon, *440*; Place des Vosges, *393*; Place Vendôme, *407*; Plan for Modernizing, *475*; Rue de Rivoli, *469*; St. Gervais, *394*; St. Séverin, *265*; St. Sulpice, *436*; Tuileries Gardens, *403*; Val-de-Grâce, *395–96*

PASSALACQUA, PIETRO (d. 1748), *428*

PAXTON, SIR JOSEPH (1803–65), *480*

PEI, I. M. (b. 1917), *529*

Peking (China): Imperial Palace, *177*; National Palace Museum, *A Pleasure Palace* (scroll), *175*

PERCIER, CHARLES (1764–1838), *469*

Pergamum (Turkey), Altar of Zeus (Berlin), *84*

Périgueux (France), Cathedral of St. Front, *221–22*

PERRAULT, CLAUDE (1613–88), *405*

PERRET, AUGUSTE (1874–1954), *506*, *519*

Persepolis (Iran): Air View and Plan, *47*; Audience Hall of Darius, *48*; Staircase to Tripylon, *48*

PERSIUS, LUDWIG (1803–45), *490*

Perugia (Italy), Porta Augusta, *87*

PERUZZI, BALDASSARE (1481–1536), *338*

Philadelphia (Pa.): Savings Fund Society Bldg., *513*; Second Bank of U.S., *473*

Phocis (Greece), Monastery of Hosios Loukas of Stiris, *142–43*

Pienza (Italy), Piazza Pio II, *311*

Pisa (Italy), Cathedral, *206–07*

POELZIG, HANS (1869–1936), *505*

Poggio a Cajano (Italy), Villa Medici, *316*

Poissy (France), Savoie House, *512*

Poitiers (France), Notre Dame la Grande, *220*

POLK, WILLIS (1867–1924), *504*

Pompeii (Italy), House of the Vettii, *110*

PÖPPELMANN, MATTHÄUS DANIEL (1662–1736), *452*

PORTA, GIACOMO DELLA (1539–1602), *350–51*

POST, PIETER (1608–69), *420*

Potsdam (Germany), Friedenskirche, *490*

Prague (Czechoslovakia): Czernin Palace, *412*; Vladislav Hall, Castle, *279*

PRANDTAUER, JAKOB (1660–1726), *447–48*

Prato (Italy), S. Maria delle Carceri, *317–18*

Priene (Turkey), Ekklesiasterion, *83*

PROMIS, CARLO (1808–72), *488*

PUGIN, A. WELBY (1812–52), *473*

Q

Qalb Lauzeh (Syria), Church, *125*

R

Racine (Wis.), Johnson Wax Bldg., *516*

RAGUZZINI, FILIPPO (c. 1680–1771), *429*

RAINALDI, CARLO (1611–91), *384*

RAPHAEL (1483–1520), *327*, *331–32*

Ravenna (Italy): S. Apollinare Nuovo, *130*; Baptistery of the Orthodox, *132–33*; Mausoleum of Galla Placidia, *129*; S. Vitale, *134–135*

Regensburg (Germany), Valhalla, *489*

Reims (France), Cathedral, *241*

Rhine River (Switzerland), Tavanasa Bridge, *500*

RICHARDSON, HENRY HOBSON (1838–86), *478–79*, *483*

RIETH, BENEDICT (fl. 1487–1502), *279*

RIETVELD, GERRIT (b. 1888), *507*

Rimini (Italy), S. Francesco, *310*

Rio de Janeiro (Brazil), Ministry of Education and Health, *517*

Ripoll (Spain), S. Maria, *201*

ROEBLING, JOHN (1806–69), *481*

ROEBLING, WASHINGTON (1837–1926), *481*

Rohr (Germany), Abbey Church, *453*

ROMANO, GIULIO (1492–1546), *336*

Rome (Italy): Basilica of Constantine, *108*; Baths of Caracalla, *106–107*; Capitol, *338–39*; Church of the Gesù, *350–51*; Colosseum, *96–97*; Forum of Trajan, *92*; Forum Romanum, *90*; Imperial Forums, *91*; Palazzo Caprini-Raphael, *332*; Palazzo Chigi-Odescalchi, *388*; Palazzo dei Tribunali, *331*; Palazzo della Consulta, *430*; Palazzo Doria-Pamphili, *430–31*; Palazzo Farnese, *333–35*; Palazzo Massimi, *338*; Palazzo Venezia, *312–13*; Palazzo Vidoni-Caffarelli, *332*; Pantheon, *101–104*; Piazza Farnese, *335*; Piazza S. Ignazio, *429*; Plan for New Avenues, *353*; Porta di Ripetta, *423*; S. Agnese in Piazza Navona, *384*; S. Andrea al Quirinale, *387*; S. Carlo alle Quattro Fontane, *380–81*; S. Caterina dei Funari, *345*; S. Costanza, *121–22*; S. Croce in Gerusalemme, *428*; S. Eligio degli Orefici, *331*; S. Giovanni in Laterano, *427*; S. Ivo della Sapienza, *382–83*; S. Maria del Priorato, *432*; S. Maria della Pace, *323*, *385*; S.

Maria Maggiore, *129*, *427*; St. Peter's, *127–28*, *326–27*, *343–44*, *374–76*, *386* (*see also* Vatican City); S. Stefano Rotondo, *124*; S. Susanna, *373*; SS. Martina e Luca, *378–79*; Spanish Stairs, *428*; Theater of Marcellus, *95*; Trevi Fountain, *422*; Villa Giulia, *341*

Ronchamp (France), Chapel of Notre Dame du Haut, *525–26*

ROOT, J. W. (1850–91), *483*

ROSSELLINO, BERNARDO (1409–64), *311*

Rotterdam (Holland): Lijnbaan, *524*; Van Nelle Factory, *508*

Rouen (France): Cathedral, *258*; St. Maclou, *264*

S

SAARINEN, EERO (1910–61), *521*

SAARINEN, ELIEL (1873–1950), *521*

St. Denis (France), Abbey Church, *232–33*, *259*

St. Gall (Switzerland), Monastery Plan, *200*

St. Louis (Mo.), Wainwright Bldg., *484*

St. Riquier (*also called* Centula; France), *196*

St. Savin sur Gartempe (France), *218*

Salem (Mass.), Pierce-Nichols House, *463*

Salisbury (England), Cathedral, *247–48*

SALVI, NICOLA (1697–1751), *422*

Salzburg (Austria), Church of the Holy Trinity, *417–18*

Samarra (Iraq), Great Mosque of Mutawakkil, *149*

San Francisco (Cal.), Hallidie Bldg., *504*

Sānchī (India): Stūpa No. 1, *162–63*; Temple No. 17, *164*

SANCTIS, FRANCESCO DE (1693–1740), *428*

SANGALLO, ANTONIO DA (1485–1546), *333–35*

SANGALLO, GIULIANO DA (1445–1516), *316–18*

SANSOVINO, JACOPO (1486–1570), *337*

SANT'ELIA, ANTONIO (1888–1917), *504*

Saqqara (Egypt): Funerary District of King Zoser, *24*; Step Pyramid of King Zoser, *23*

Säynätsalo (Finland), Civic Center, *524*

SCAMOZZI, VINCENZO (1552–1616), *354*

SCHINKEL, KARL F. (1781–1841), *489*

SCHLUETER, ANDREAS (c. 1664–1714), *413*

Schwäbisch Gmünd, *see* Gmünd, Schwäbisch

Sées (France), Cathedral of Notre Dame, 263
SERVANDONI, JEAN-NICOLAS (1695–1766), 436
Siena (Italy): Cathedral, 253; City Plan, 256; Town Hall, 256
SILOE, DIEGO DA (c. 1495–1563), 364
SIXTUS V, POPE (1521–90), 353
SKIDMORE, OWINGS & MERRILL (architectural firm), 523, 528
SMIRKE, SIR ROBERT (1781–1867), 471
SOHIER, HECTOR (fl. 1528–45), 360
SOUFFLOT, JACQUES GERMAIN (1713–80), 440
SPECCHI, ALESSANDRO (1668–1729), 423
Speyer (Germany), Cathedral, 230
Split (Yugoslavia), Palace of Diocletian, 115–17
Stockholm (Sweden): City Hall, 496; Woodland Crematorium, 514
Stonehenge (England), 18
STRICKLAND, WILLIAM (1788–1854), 473
Stupinigi (Italy), Royal Hunting Palace, 424–25
SULLIVAN, LOUIS (1856–1924), 484–85
Susa (Italy), Monumental Arch, 109
SUSTRIS, FRIEDRICH (c. 1540–99), 368
Sydenham (England), Crystal Palace II, 480

T

Tabriz (Iran), Masjid-i-Ali Shah, 158
Tel-el-Amarna (Egypt): House of Vizier Nakht, 34; Houses on Edge of Wady, 35; Official Central Quarter, 34
Teotihuacan (Mexico): Detail of Southwest Area, 180; Pyramid of the Sun, 179; Temple of Quetzalcoatl, 181
Tiahuanaco (Bolivia), "Gate of the Sun," 188
Timgad (Algeria), City Plan, 89
Tiryns (Greece), Palace and Citadel, 55
Tivoli (Italy): Hadrian's Villa, 113–14; Temple of the Sibyl, 94; Villa d'Este, 340
Todi (Italy), S. Maria della Consolazione, 328–30
Tokyo (Japan), National Museum of: Construction Methods, 173; House of a Priest, 174;

House of a Lesser Nobleman, 174
TOLEDO, JUAN BAUTISTA DE (d. 1567), 365–66
Tomar (Portugal), Cristo Monastery, 366
Torralba (Sardinia), Nuraghe Sant'Antine, 20
TORRALVA, DIOGO DE (1500–66), 366
Toulouse (France): Church of the Jacobins, 262; St. Sernin, 223–24
Tournai (France), Cathedral, 231
Tournus (France), St. Philibert, 216–17
Trier (Germany): Basilica, 126; Liebfrauenkirche, 249–50; Porta Nigra, 120
Turin (Italy): Cathedral, 390; Church of the Carmine, 426; Exhibition Hall, 522; Palazzo Carignano, 391–92; Piazza Vittorio Veneto, 488; St. Lorenzo, 389; Superga, 423
Twickenham (England), Strawberry Hill, 446

U

Uji (Japan), Hōōdō, Byodoin Temple, 172
Ulm (Germany), Münster, 276–77, 279
UPJOHN, RICHARD (1802–78), 474
Uronarti Island (Egypt), Fortress, 28
Uruk (Iraq), "White Temple," 40
Utrecht (Holland), Schröder House, 507
Uxmal (Mexico), Nunnery Quadrangle, 184

V

Valencia (Spain), Palace of the Marqués de Dos Aguas, 460
Valladolid (Spain), S. Gregorio, 281
VALVASSORI, GABRIELI (1683–1771), 430–31
VAN DEN BROEK & BAKEMA (architectural firm), 522
VAN EYCK, JAN (c. 1370–1440), 245
VANBRUGH, SIR JOHN (1664–1726), 445–46
VANVITELLI, LUIGI (1700–73), 432–33
VASARI, GIORGIO (1511–74), 341–42
VASQUEZ, F. MANUEL (1697–1765), 459
Vatican City (Rome): Belvedere

Court, 325; Basilica of St. Peter, 326–27, 343–44, 374–76, 386
Vaux-le-Vicomte (France), Château of, 398
VELDE, HENRY VAN DE (1863–1957), 501–02
Venice (Italy): Ca' d'Oro, 290; Basilica of St. Mark, 208–10; Library of St. Mark, 337; S. Giorgio Maggiore, 347–48; S. Maria della Salute, 377; S. Zaccaria, 322
VERGARA, IGNACIO (1715–76), 460
Versailles (France): Château of, 399–402, 404; Le Hameau, 441; Petit Trianon, 439
Vicenza (Italy): Teatro Olimpico, 349; Villa Rotonda, 346
Vienna (Austria): Belvedere, Upper Palace, 451; Post Office Savings Bank, 496; St. Charles Borromaeus, 449–50; Steiner House, 498; Votivkirche, 491
VIGNOLA, GIACOMO (1507–73), 341, 350–51
VILLARD DE HONNECOURT, see HONNECOURT
VINCI, LEONARDO DA (1452–1519), 320
VITTONE, BERNARDO (1704/5–70), 434–35
VLADIMIR (U.S.S.R.), Church of the Dormition, 144
VLUGT, L. C. VAN DER (b. 1894), 508
VOYSEY, CHARLES F. A. (1857–1941), 479

W

WAGNER, OTTO (1841–1918), 496
WALPOLE, HORACE (1717–97) 446
Washington (D.C.), City Plan, 464
Wells (England), Cathedral, 271
Westover (Va.), Byrd House, 461
"Wies, Die" (Germany), 448
Winchester (England), Cathedral, 225
WOOD, JOHN, THE ELDER (1704–54), 442
WOOD, JOHN, THE YOUNGER (1728–81), 442
WREN, SIR CHRISTOPHER (1632–1723), 409–11
WRIGHT, FRANK LLOYD (1867–1959), 499, 515–16
Würzburg (Germany), Episcopal Palace, 454–55

Z

ZIMMERMANN, DOMINIKUS (1685–1766), 458

LIST OF ABBREVIATED SOURCES
IN THE LIST OF ILLUSTRATIONS

ACL *(Archives centrales iconographiques, Brussels);* AEROFILMS *(Aerofilms, Ltd., London);* ALINARI *(Fratelli Alinari, Florence);* ALTEROCCA *(Alterocca, Terni);* ANDERSON *(See Alinari);* ANDREWS *(Wayne Andrews, Brooklyn, N. Y.);* ARAGOZZINI *(Foto Aragozzini, Milan);* ARCH. PHOT. *(Archives Photographiques, Paris);* ARCH. T.C.I. *(Archivio Touring Club Italiano, Milan);* BENEVOLO *(Professor Leonardo Benevolo, Rome);* BISSANTZ *(Edgar Bissantz, Carmel, Cal.);* BLONDEL *(J. F. Blondel,* Architecture Française, *Paris, 1752–56);* B.O.N. *(Bildarchiv Oesterreichische Nationalbibliothek, Vienna);* BUCKLEY *(Raymond R. Buckley, Boston);* CAF *(Compagnie Aérienne Française, Suresnes);* CHEVOJON *(Chevojon, Paris);* CONANT *(Kenneth John Conant,* Carolingian and Romanesque Architecture, *800–1200, Baltimore, 1959);* COURTAULD INST. *(Courtauld Institute, University of London, London);* DEGENHART *(Dr. B. Degenhart, Munich);* DINSMOOR *(W. B. Dinsmoor,* Architecture of Ancient Greece, *New York, 1950, 3rd. ed.);* DKV *(Deutscher Kunstverlag, Munich);* DUCERCEAU *(J. A. Ducerceau,* Livre d'Architecture, *Paris, 1559);* EDIZIONE E.S. *(Edizione E.S., Ravenna);* ELISOFON *(Eliot Elisofon,* © *Time, Inc., New York);* FELTON *(Leo Herbert-Felton, London);* FIORENTINI *(Fiorentini, Venice);* FOKKER *(Timon H. Fokker,* Roman Baroque Art, *London, 1938);* FOND. CINI *(Fondazione Giorgio Cini, Venice);* FOTOCIELO *(Fotocielo, Rome);* FOTOTECA UNIONE *(Fototeca Unione, Via Angelo Masina 5, Rome);* FOUCAULT *(Marc Foucault, Paris);* FOX *(Fox Photos, London);* FRANTZ *(Alison Frantz, Princeton, N. J.);* GAI *(German Archaeological Institute);* GEBR. METZ *(Gebrüder Metz, Tübingen);* GERNSHEIM *(Collection Helmut Gernsheim, London);* GFN *(Gabinetto Fotografico Nazionale, Rome);* GIRAUDON *(Giraudon, Paris);* GNS *(Gabinetto Nazionale delle Stampe, Rome);* GUILLÈN *(Abraham Guillèn, Lima);* HABS *(Historic American Buildings Survey, Smithsonian Institute, Washington, D. C.);* HEGE *(Professor Walter Hege, Hege-Archiv, Karlsruhe);* HERRARD *(Herrard, Paris);* HERVÉ *(Lucien Hervé, Paris);* HILL *(I. T. Hill,* Ancient City of Athens, *Cambridge, 1953);* HIRMER *(Dr. Max Hirmer, Hirmer Verlag, Munich);* HITCHCOCK *(Henry Russell Hitchcock,* Architecture: Nineteenth and Twentieth Centuries, *Baltimore, 1958);* HURAULT *(Charles Hurault, Paris);* I.G.N. *(Institut Géographique National, Paris);* JEITER *(J. Jeiter, Hadamar, Germany);* KEETMAN *(Peter Keetman, Breitbrunn/Chiemsee, Germany);* KERSTING *(A. F. Kersting, London);* KIDDER SMITH *(G. E. Kidder Smith, New York);* KPV *(Kunsthistorischer Photo-Verlag Neubacher);* LANGE AND HIRMER *(Kurt Lange and Max Hirmer,* Aegypten, *Munich, 1955);* LASTEYRIE *(R. C. Lasteyrie du Saillant,* L'Architecture Religieuse en France à l'époque gothique, *Paris, 1926–27);* LAWRENCE *(A. W. Lawrence,* Greek Architecture, *Baltimore, 1957);* LETAROUILLY, LE VATICAN... *(Paul M. Letarouilly,* Le Vatican et la Basilique de Saint-Pierre à Rome, *Paris, 1882);* LETAROUILLY, LES EDIFICES... *(Paul M. Letarouilly,* Les Edifices de Rome Moderne, *Paris, 1856);* LIST *(Herbert List, Munich);* LURÇAT *(A. Lurçat,* Formes, composition, et lois d'harmonie, *Paris, 1955);* MAIURI *(A. Maiuri,* Arte e civiltà nell'Italia antica, *Milan, 1960);* MARBURG *(Bildarchiv Foto Marburg, Marburg/Lahn);* MARCEL *(Jean-Marie Marcel, Paris);* MAS *(A. y R. Mas, Barcelona);* MASSON *(Georgina Masson, courtesy Thames & Hudson, Ltd., London);* MONCALVO *(Moncalvo, Turin);* MÜLLER *(Erich Müller, Kassel);* MW *(Ministry of Works, London, Crown Copyright);* NBR *(Copyright National Buildings Record, London);* NEUERBERG *(Norman Neuerberg, Fototeca Unione, Rome);* NICKEL *(Richard Nickel, Park Ridge, Ill.);* OR. INST. *(Oriental Institute, University of Chicago, Chicago, Ill.);* PATTE *(Pierre Patte,* Monuments érigés à la gloire de Louis XV, *Paris, 1765);* PEDRINI *(Pedrini, Turin);* POLLITZER *(Eric Pollitzer, New York);* POPE *(Professor Arthur Upham Pope, Cornwall Bridge, Conn.);* RCHM *(Royal Commission on Historic Monuments, London, Crown Copyright);* RENGER-PATZSCH *(A. Renger-Patzsch, Wamel-Dorf über Soest i. W., Germany);* ROLLIE McKENNA *(Rollie McKenna, New York);* ROUBIER *(Jean Roubier, Paris);* SANDERSON AND DIXON *(Sanderson and Dixon, Ambleside);* SBB *(Formerly Staatliche Bildstelle, Berlin; now available through Deutscher Kunstverlag, Munich);* SCHAEFER *(J. H. Schaefer & Son, Baltimore, Md.);* SCHLEGEL *(Dr. Arthur Schlegel, Munich);* SCHMIDT-GLASSNER *(Helga Schmidt-Glassner, Stuttgart);* SCHNEIDERS, TONI *(Toni Schneiders, Lindau-Schachen);* SCRANTON *(Robert L. Scranton,* Greek Architecture, *New York, 1962);* SIBBELEE *(Hans Sibbelee, Nederhorst den Berg);* SMITH, EDWIN *(Edwin Smith, London);* SOPR. GAL. FLOR. *(Soprintendenza alle Gallerie, Florence);* SOPR. MON. LAZ. *(Soprintendenza ai Monumenti del Lazio, Rome);* SOPR. MON. PIED. *(Soprintendenza ai Monumenti del Piemonte, Turin);* STEGMANN AND GEYMÜLLER *(C. M. Stegmann and H. von Geymüller,* The Architecture of the Renaissance in Tuscany, *New York, 1924);* STOEDTNER *(Dr. Franz Stoedtner, Düsseldorf);* TASS *(Tass Agency, Moscow);* THAMES & HUDSON *(Thames and Hudson, Ltd., London);* VAJENTI *(Vajenti, Vicenza);* VINCENT *(John B. Vincent, Berkeley, Cal.);* VIZZAVONA *(Vizzavona, Paris);* VON MATT *(Leonard von Matt, Buochs);* WARD *(Clarence Ward, Oberlin, Ohio);* YAN *(Yan Photo Reportage, Toulouse).*